Economic Literacy

By

SCHYRLET CAMERON, JANIE DOSS, AND SUZANNE MYERS

COPYRIGHT © 2008 Mark Twain Media, Inc.

ISBN 978-1-58037-470-5

Printing No. CD-404096

Mark Twain Media, Inc., Publishers
Distributed by Carson-Dellosa Publishing LLC

Visit us at www.carsondellosa.com

Table of Contents

Introduction

Economic Literacy is designed to help students gain a better understanding of how the American economic system works. Difficult and confusing economic terms and concepts are presented in a simplified format, making them easy to teach and learn.

Lessons offer students an opportunity to practice research skills and access information through technology. Real-life activities allow students to explore economic concepts. This results in meaningful learning that promotes economic literacy. Each lesson contains the following sections:

- The **reading exercise** introduces students to a specific economic concept while building vocabulary.

- The **Assessment** evaluates student comprehension of information in the reading exercise.

- The **Historical Connection** activities are teacher-directed primary source activities that provide a connection between economic concepts and historical events.

- **Knowledge Builders** are challenging teacher-directed activities, simulations, and games that reinforce learning of core economic concepts.

- The **Teacher Resource Bank** contains useful information for teachers. Lessons are correlated to the National Council on Economics Education (NCEE) Standards and the National Educational Technology Standards (NETS). A list of suggested resources and related web sites have been provided for further research and reference.

Economic Literacy supports the Excellence in Economic Education (EEE) Act, which is a component of the No Child Left Behind (NCLB) Act. The primary purpose of the EEE Act is "the improvement of the quality of student understanding of personal finance and economics." The Education Through Technology Act of 2001 is also a component of NCLB. Its purpose is to integrate technology into the elementary and secondary curriculum and instruction.

Bartering

Early Forms of Bartering

Thousands of years ago, ancient people did not use money. They lived by hunting and gathering food. As people learned how to domesticate plants and animals, a **surplus**, or overabundance, of food was created. This surplus allowed people to barter. **Bartering** is the trading of items people have for the items they need or want.

Bartering in the New World

Early explorers of the New World found Native Americans willing to trade furs for blankets, metal tools, and trinkets. The trapping and trading of furs became a **profitable**, or moneymaking, business. The Hudson Bay Company set up trading posts in Canada and later expanded into U.S. territory. As the demand for furs increased, European trappers competed with Native Americans in the hunt for fur-bearing animals.

Settlement of the New World led to many interesting exchanges between settlers and Native Americans. As settlements grew, the demand for land increased. The settlers often traded with the Native Americans to acquire more land. One famous act of bartering occurred in the early 1600s. Dutch settlers were able to swap $24.00 worth of trading goods with the Native Americans for the island that is now Manhattan.

Bartering in Colonial and Revolutionary America

Bartering played a major role in the economy of colonial America. The colonists found bartering with items they had access to, such as tobacco and corn, an acceptable way to pay debts and buy goods within the colonies. During the American Revolution, colonists were once again forced to rely on bartering. Even George Washington found it necessary to barter to obtain supplies for the Continental Army.

The nation grew after winning its independence. As settlers pushed further and further west, bartering helped explorers and settlers build friendly relationships with the Native Americans. The journals of the Lewis and Clark Expedition contain many accounts of bartering with Native Americans.

Modern-Day Bartering

Bartering is still an important economic tool. Many people, communities, and nations find bartering useful in acquiring the things they need and want. In order to save money, companies and individuals have discovered the convenience of online bartering.

Name: _____ Date: _____

Assessment

Matching

_____ 1. surplus

_____ 2. barter

_____ 3. profitable

a. moneymaking business

b. overabundance or having more than needed

c. trading items people have for items they need or want

Fill in the Blanks

1. As people learned how to domesticate plants and animals, a _____ of food was created.

2. The _____ _____ Company set up trading posts in Canada and later expanded into U.S. territory.

3. George Washington found it necessary to barter for supplies for the

   _____ _____.

4. Dutch settlers were able to swap $24.00 worth of trading goods with the Native Americans for the island that is now _____.

5. The journals of the _____ and _____ Expedition contain accounts of bartering with Native Americans.

Constructed Response

Explain what bartering is and how people use it today. Give specific examples and details to support your answer.

_____

_____

_____

_____

_____

Historical Connection

Activity One

Primary Source:

<http://memory.loc.gov/cgi-bin/query/r?ammem/mgw:@field(DOCID+@lit(gw100454))>
   Fitzpatrick, John C. editor. "George Washington to William Smallwood, February 21, 1778." *The George Washington Papers at the Library of Congress, 1741-1799.* The Library of Congress.

Directions: George Washington realized he could not rely on the Continental Congress to provide his army with the equipment and materials needed to fight the Revolutionary War. Most of his men lacked the basic supplies needed to survive the harsh winter at Valley Forge. Students examine the primary source, George Washington's letter to William Smallwood. Using their knowledge of bartering and the information in the primary source, students role-play William Smallwood bartering with merchants to purchase the hides requested by Washington.

Activity Two

Primary Source:

<http://www.xmission.com/~drudy/mtman/html/ashlist.html>
   "Inventory of Goods at the 1825 Rendezvous on Henry's Fork of the Green River (cached goods listed in Ashley's diary)." *Fur Trade Business Records.* American Mountain Men.

Directions: Mountain men looked forward to the annual rendezvous held each summer. During the two-week event, traders, trappers, and Native Americans gathered to exchange furs for supplies. Students examine the primary source, a list of supplies William Ashley took to the 1825 rendezvous on Henry's Fork of the Green River. Students research mountain men, the fur trade industry, and the history of the rendezvous. Using their research, students create a list of supplies needed to survive for a winter in the Rocky Mountains while hunting and trapping.

Activity Three

Primary Source:

<http://www.xmission.com/~drudy/mtman/html/ads.html>
   "Want Ads for Mountain Men." *Miscellaneous Items of Interest From Western Fur Trade History.* American Mountain Men.

Directions: Fur-trading companies hired men to hunt and trap. These trappers became known as "mountain men." Students examine the primary source to discover job opportunities for men in the Rocky Mountains. Students research "mountain men" to identify the skills needed to be a successful hunter and trapper. Using their research, teams of students create a help-wanted advertisement for the Rocky Mountain Fur Company.

DAILY WANT ADS
EMPLOYMENT OPPORTUNITIES
200 MEN NEEDED
TRAPPERS - TOP PAY!

Knowledge Builder

Trading Day

Students hold a "Trading Day" to experience bartering. Each student will receive a bag containing an assortment of individually wrapped candy. The amount of candy in the bags will vary. One or two students will receive bags containing a popular candy bar. Students barter with other students using candy from their bags to make trades. After several minutes, stop the bartering and allow students to discuss any difficulties they experienced while bartering.

Rendezvous Simulation

Directions: Divide the class into two groups: traders and mountain men. Give each trader a *Trading Company Price List*. Each mountain man needs one of the individual *Mountain Man Supply Lists* and a copy of the *Animal Pelts* page. Seat the traders randomly around the room and post a copy of the *Trading Company Price List*. Following the *Rendezvous Rules*, mountain men will trade with traders to acquire items on their supply list. To complete a successful trade, the mountain man will give the correct number of pelt cards to the trader. Students will quickly realize they do not have enough beaver pelt cards. They will need to barter with other mountain men to acquire the pelt cards needed to completely fill their supply lists. After several minutes, stop the trading and find out which students were able to completely fill their supply lists. Have students discuss the bartering experience and the pros and cons of bartering.

Rendezvous Rules:

1. Do not interrupt a barter in progress.
2. Do not barter with more than one person at a time.
3. Be polite even when someone chooses not to barter with you.

Mountain Man Supply Lists
Directions: Give one supply list to each student portraying a mountain man. Duplicate supply lists based on the number of students portraying mountain men.

Supply List 1:	bag of flour, bag of coffee, bag of sugar, knife, flint
Supply List 2:	horseshoes, fish hooks, bag of sugar, bag of flour, bag of coffee
Supply List 3:	bag of sugar, bag of flour, beaver trap, bag of coffee, kettle
Supply List 4:	blanket, scissors, saddle, bag of salt, bag of coffee
Supply List 5:	lead for bullets, bag of gunpowder, bar of soap, pistol, bag of flour
Supply List 6:	thread, bridle, needles, bag of flour, bag of sugar

Rendezvous Simulation (cont.)

Animal Pelts

Directions: Each student portraying a mountain man in the Rendezvous Simulation will need a copy of this page. Students cut apart the animal pelt trading cards.

Muskrat	**Lynx**	**Otter**	**Mink**
Muskrat	**Lynx**	**Otter**	**Mink**
Muskrat	**Lynx**	**Otter**	**Mink**
Beaver	**Lynx**	**Otter**	**Mink**
Beaver	**Beaver**	**Beaver**	**Beaver**
Beaver	**Beaver**	**Beaver**	**Beaver**

Rendezvous Simulation (cont.)

Trading Company Price List

Directions: Give each student portraying a trader in the Rendezvous Simulation a *Trading Company Price List*.

Supplies	Prices in Number of Pelts				
	Beaver	Mink	Lynx	Otter	Muskrat
Bag of Flour	2	3	4	5	6
Bag of Coffee	2	3	4	5	6
Bag of Sugar	2	3	4	5	6
Knife	3	4	5	6	7
Flint	2	3	4	5	6
Horseshoes	3	3	4	5	6
Fish Hooks	2	3	4	5	6
Beaver Trap	4	5	6	7	8
Kettle	3	4	5	6	7
Blanket	3	4	5	6	7
Scissors	1	2	3	4	5
Saddle	4	5	6	7	8
Bag of Salt	1	2	3	4	5
Lead for Bullets	1	2	3	4	5
Bag of Gunpowder	3	4	5	6	7
Bar of Soap	1	2	3	4	5
Pistol	5	6	7	8	9
Thread	2	3	4	5	6
Bridle	3	4	5	6	7
Needles	2	3	4	5	6

Teacher Resource Bank

National Standards Correlation:

NCEE Standard 5 (Gain From Trade): Voluntary exchange occurs only when all participating parties expect to gain. This is true for trade among individuals or organizations within a nation, and usually among individuals or organizations in different nations.

NET Standard 5 (Technology Research Tools): Students use technology to locate, evaluate, and collect information from a variety of sources.

Bookshelf Resources:

Cooper, Jason. *Money Through the Ages.* Rourke Publishing Group, 2003.

Loewen, Nancy. *Let's Trade: A Book About Bartering.* Picture Window Books, 2006.

Santella, Andrew. *Mountain Men.* Children's Press, 2003.

Suen, Anastasia. *Trappers & Mountain Men.* Rourke Publishing Group, 2007.

Sundling, Charles W. *Mountain Men of the Frontier.* Abdo Publishing Group, 2000.

Online Resources:

<http://www.nps.gov/nr/travel/kingston/colonization.htm>
   "Dutch Colonies." *Kingston: A National Register of Historic Places Travel Itinerary.* National Park Service.

<http://www.nps.gov/archive/jeff/LewisClark2/Circa1804/In1804/HeadlinesLouisiana Purchase.htm>
   Jefferson National Expansion Memorial. *The United States Takes Possession of the Louisiana Territory.* National Park Service.

<http://lewisandclarkjournals.unl.edu/>
   The Journals of the Lewis and Clark Expedition. University of Nebraska-Lincoln.

<http://xroads.virginia.edu/~hyper/HNS/Mtmen/home.html>
   Zimmerman, Emily. *The Mountain Men: Pathfinders of the West 1810-1860.* The University of Virginia.

History of Money

From Bartering to Currency

As civilizations grew, bartering became an increasingly more difficult economic system to use. People began using items such as shells, salt, and cattle as the **unit of exchange**, or the first money. Gradually, a money economy replaced the barter system for most of the world.

When trade and travel expanded beyond the local community, people sought a **commodity**, or common item, that everyone would accept for payment. Lumps of precious metal became a standard unit of exchange. Gold and silver were the most commonly used metals because

they were durable and could be divided into smaller pieces. Coins made from precious metals were first used in Turkey, Egypt, Greece, and Rome. However, carrying around bags of coins eventually became too burdensome, so a more convenient form of money evolved. The Chinese were the first civilization to use paper money; later, European countries adopted the custom.

Currency in the New World

The first settlers to the New World brought little money with them. England prohibited the colonies from producing currency. This was a way to force the colonies to trade exclusively with England. At first, the settlers used corn, tobacco, and other goods as money. Massachusetts was the first colony to make its own coins and paper money. Later, other colonial governments issued their own currency. However, paper money is only good if there is enough gold or silver to exchange for it. Soon, the colonies had more money in circulation than they had gold or silver. This made the colonial money worthless.

Continentals and Greenbacks

Enthusiasm for printing paper money continued to cause problems for Americans. During the American Revolution, the Continental Congress issued **continentals**, or the paper money of the national government, to finance the war. The United States government also issued paper money, nicknamed **greenbacks**, during the Civil War to pay debts. Both times, the paper money became worthless because there wasn't enough gold or silver to back the new money. During these times, banks were also allowed to issue paper money.

To establish better control over the supply of money in circulation, Congress passed the Federal Reserve Act in 1913. The United States Treasury bought up all the paper money in circulation. Federal Reserve Banks, established under the new law, were the only banks

authorized to issue paper money. The Federal Reserve Banks were also given the job of managing the nation's money supply. Today, Federal Reserve notes, our current paper money, are printed by the Bureau of Engraving and Printing. These notes are **legal tender**, or the official money used for payment, for all debts in the United States.

Name: _____ Date: _____

Assessment

Matching

_____ 1. commodity
_____ 2. legal tender

_____ 3. continentals
_____ 4. greenbacks

a. paper money issued by the Continental Congress
b. paper money issued by the U.S. government during the Civil War
c. a common item accepted as payment
d. the official money of a government

Fill in the Blank

1. As civilizations grew, _____ became an increasingly more difficult economic system to use.

2. When trade and travel expanded beyond the local community, people sought a common _____ that everyone would accept for payment.

3. The _____ were the first civilization to use paper money.

4. _____ was the first colony to make its own coins and paper money.

5. During the American Revolution, the Continental Congress issued paper money, or _____, to finance the war.

6. To establish better control over the supply of money in circulation, Congress passed the _____ _____ Act of 1913.

Constructed Response

The United States is composed of 50 states, each with its own state government, but only the United States Congress has the power to issue currency. Explain why it is important that state governments are not allowed to make and distribute their own money. Give specific examples and details to support your answer.

_____

_____

_____

_____

_____

Historical Connection

Activity One

Primary Source:
<http://memory.loc.gov/cgi-bin/query/r?ammen/hlaw:@field(DOCID+@lit(dg00686))>
> "John Hancock to Philip Schuyler." *Letters of Delegates to Congress: Volume 6 January 1, 1777 - April 30, 1777.* The Library of Congress.

Directions: During the Revolutionary War, each state printed its own paper money. This caused the overprinting of currency, leading to the "depreciation of the Continental Currency." In a letter, John Hancock called the depreciation a "growing Evil." During the Civil War, overprinting of greenbacks led to the same problem. Students research the history of the continental and the greenback. Using their research, students construct a Venn diagram comparing the conditions leading to the depreciation of the continentals and greenbacks.

Knowledge Builder

The History of Money

No one knows positively where or when money was first used. The Mesopotamians are believed to be one of the first civilizations to use metal as money. Students research the history of money. Using the information, they generate a time line identifying important events in the history of money. Some possible research questions to guide the students include:

1. Which civilization first minted money?
2. Which civilization gave money its name?
3. Which civilization was the first to use paper money?
4. Which American colony first printed paper money?

The First Money

Almost everything that was easy to carry around and easy to count was first used as money. People used seeds, seashells, and even rocks. Students research the history of money to discover objects once used as money. Using their research, students create a display of the items and identify the societies that used them as money.

Names of Money

Money has been known by many names. For example, a piece of eight was a Spanish silver coin and wampum was beads made of shells. Students compile a list of words or phrases that have been used as synonyms for money.

Teacher Resource Bank

National Standards Correlation:
NCEE Standard 11 (Role of Money): Money makes it easier to trade, borrow, save, invest, and compare the value of goods and services.

NET Standard 5 (Technology Research Tools): Students use technology to locate, evaluate, and collect information from a variety of sources.

Bookshelf Resources:
Drobot, Eve. *Money, Money, Money: Where It Comes From, How to Save It, Spend It, and Make It.* Maple Tree Press, 2004.

Giesecke, Ernestine. *From Seashells to Smart Cards: Money and Currency.* Heinemann Library, 2003.

Kummer, Patricia K. *Inventions that Shaped the World: Currency.* Scholastic, 2004.

Maestro, Betty. *The Story of Money.* Mulberry Books, 1995.

Online Resources:
<http://www.frbsf.org/currency/>
   American Currency Exhibit. Federal Reserve Bank of San Francisco.

<http://www.usmint.gov/kids>
   h.i.p. Pocket Change. The United States Mint.

<http://www.pbs.org/newshour/on2/money/history.html>
   "History of Money." *Newshour Extra: A Newshour with Jim Lehrer Special for Students.* 2005. Public Broadcasting Service.

<http://minneapolisfed.org/econed/curric/history.cfm>
   The History of Money. Federal Reserve Bank of Minneapolis.

<http://www.pbs.org/wgbh/nova/moolah/history.html>
   "The History of Money." *Nova Online: Secrets of Making Money.* August 2002. Public Broadcasting Service.

<http://www.bep.treas.gov/section.cfm.4>
   "U.S. Banknotes: Safer. Smarter. More Secure." The Bureau of Engraving and Printing.

United States Currency

The Department of the Treasury

In 1788, the Constitution was adopted. It gave Congress the sole authority to mint coins and control their value. Congress established the United States Department of the Treasury in 1789. Alexander Hamilton served as the first Secretary of the Treasury. The Department of the Treasury was given the job of overseeing the production of coins and currency notes. Two agencies of the Department of the Treasury are responsible for manufacturing the currency: The United States Mint and The Bureau of Engraving and Printing.

The United States Mint

In 1792, Congress passed The Coinage Act, which created the United States Mint. The Mint is the federal agency responsible for the production and distribution of coins. The Mint once produced gold and silver coins. Today, coins are made of copper, nickel, and an **alloy**, which is a mixture of metals. Coins are **minted**, or manufactured, in six different **denominations**, or amounts. The denominations are the penny, nickel, dime, quarter, half-dollar, and dollar. Mints in Denver and Philadelphia make most of the coins for circulation. Coins are marked with a "D" or "P" to identify their minting location. However, coins minted in Philadelphia do not always bear a mintmark.

The Federal Reserve

Originally, paper money was backed by silver or gold. Anyone could take a one-dollar bill to a bank and exchange it for silver or gold. As the amount of money in circulation increased, paper money outgrew the nation's supply of silver and gold. The Federal Reserve Act of 1913 was passed in order to manage the nation's monetary policy and to supervise the banking system. This act established the Federal Reserve System, known as the Fed. The Federal Reserve System consists of 12 regional banks. The Fed has strict control over the amount of money that is circulated.

The Bureau of Engraving and Printing

In 1862, Congress authorized the Bureau of Engraving and Printing to design, engrave, and print the official paper money of the United States. Today, Federal Reserve notes are

the legal tender of the United States. The notes are issued in the amounts of $1, $2, $5, $10, $20, $50, and $100. Features on each denomination will vary, but printed on each bill are the words "Federal Reserve Note," a green Treasury seal, and the identifying markings of the issuing Federal Reserve Bank.

Name: _____ Date: _____

Assessment

Matching

_____ 1. alloy
_____ 2. minted
_____ 3. denominations
_____ 4. Federal Reserve Notes

a. legal tender of the United States
b. amounts
c. manufactured coins
d. a mixture of metals

Fill in the Blanks

1. The United States _____ gave Congress the sole authority to mint coins and control their value.

2. _____ _____ served as the first Secretary of the Treasury.

3. Coins are marked with a "D" or _____ to identify their minting location.

4. The Federal Reserve Act of 1913 established the _____ _____ System, known as the Fed.

5. The notes are issued in the amounts of $_____, $_____, $5, $10, $20, $50, and $_____.

Constructed Response

What are the names of the two agencies responsible for the manufacturing of U.S. currency? List the responsibilities of each agency.

_____

_____

_____

_____

_____

_____

Historical Connection

Activity One

Primary Source:
<http://memory.loc.gov/cgi-bin/query/r?ammem/rbpe:@field(DOCID+@lit(rbpe23300900))>
Snowden, James Ross. "Circular: Mint of the United States, Philadelphia, July 26th, 1853." *An American Time Capsule: Three Centuries of Broadsides and Other Printed Ephemera.* The Library of Congress.

Directions: In 1853, artists and engravers were invited to submit designs for silver coins. Three designs were to be selected. Examine the primary source to determine the reason the Director of the Mint did not give any suggestions for the design of the coins. Students pretend they have received an invitation from the current director of the Mint to submit a design for a new coin. Each student submits an entry to the Mint that includes a drawing of the obverse (front) and reverse (back) side of the coin, along with a written explanation for the symbolism incorporated into the design.

Activity Two

Primary Source:
<http://memory.loc.gov/cgi-bin/query/r?ammem/bdsdcc:@field(DOCID+@lit(bdsdcc13001))>
"Propositions respecting the coinage of gold, silver, and copper." *Documents from the Continental Congress and the Constitutional Convention, 1774-1789.* The Library of Congress.

Directions: On July 6, 1785, the Continental Congress approved the dollar "as the unit of coinage, and the decimal ratio." This vote was brought about after the submission of a report from the Grand Committee of the Continental Congress, a plan by Robert Morris, and notes submitted by Thomas Jefferson. Students examine the section of the primary source that are the notes submitted by Thomas Jefferson and then answer the following Document-Based Questions (DBQs) on their own paper.

1. What are the three factors that Thomas Jefferson said were of primary importance when fixing the unit of money?

2. What foreign coin did Jefferson believe fulfilled these conditions?

3. What was his reasoning for sticking with the dollar for "the unit"?

Knowledge Builder

Features on the Coins

Students examine a variety of coins to become familiar with the identifying features. Divide students into teams. Give each team several magnifying glasses and a sealed plastic bag containing an assortment of coins. Students examine each side of the coins. One side of the coin often features the portrait of a deceased person who has had a positive impact on United States history. This side is known as the **obverse** side. The other side, or **reverse**, usually features a unique design and the monetary value of the coin. Other items to look for include: motto, mintmark, and the date of issue.

Obverse   Reverse

Numismatist

A **numismatist** is a coin collector. There are many types of coin collections. Some examples of coin collections include rare or hard-to-find coins, imperfect coins or coins with printing mistakes, and coin sets. Have students start their own collections. First, they choose a theme for their collection, such as a coin of each denomination minted in their birth year, or pennies in a yearly progression starting with their birth year. On a 2 x 2-inch square of white paper, students make coin rubbings of the obverse (front) and reverse (back) sides of a coin by placing the paper square over a coin and rubbing the surface with firm pencil strokes. Students follow this procedure for as many different coins as they have. They then arrange and attach the rubbings on poster board.

Teacher Resource Bank

National Standards Correlation:
NCEE Standard 11 (Role of Money): Money makes it easier to trade, borrow, save, invest, and compare the value of goods and services.

NET Standard 5 (Technology Research Tools): Students use technology to locate, evaluate, and collect information from a variety of sources.

Bookshelf Resources:
Allman, Barbara. *Banking.* Lerner Publications, 2005.

Attebury, Nancy Garhan. *Out and About at the United States Mint.* Picture Window Books, 2005.

Cooper, Jason. *U.S. Treasury.* Rourke Publishing Group, 1999.

Giesecke, Ernestine. *From Seashells to Smart Cards: Money and Currency.* Heinemann Library, 2003.

Parker, Nancy Winslow. *Money, Money, Money: The Meaning of the Art and Symbols on United States Paper Currency.* HarperCollins Children's Books, 1995.

Online Resources:
<http://www.frbsf.org/currency/>
   American Currency Exhibit. Federal Reserve Bank of San Francisco.

<http://www.moneyfactory.gov/newmoney/main/cfm/learning/fun>
   "Fun and Games." *Youth Education.* 2007. The Bureau of Engraving and Printing.

<http://www.moneyfactory.gov/document.cfm/18/106>
   "Fun Facts." *Money Facts.* 2007. The Bureau of Engraving and Printing.

<http://www.usmint.gov/kids>
   h.i.p. Pocket Change. The United States Mint.

<http://www.secretservice.gov/know_your_money.shtml>
   "History of United States Currency." *Know Your Money.* 2006. United States Secret Service.

<http://www.pbs.org/wgbh/nova/moolah/history.html>
   Nova Online: Secrets of Making Money. August 2002. Public Broadcasting Service.

Features of Money

Functions of Money

Our money has three main functions. First, it is used as a **medium of exchange**, meaning people will accept it in exchange for goods or services. Second, it can be used as a **unit of accounting**, which allows people to use it to keep records. Third, it has a **store of value**, meaning people can save it for future purchases.

Characteristics of Money

Anything that people are willing to accept in payment for goods and services can function as money. There are certain characteristics that an object must have to be classified as money.

Characteristic	Description
accepted	People will accept it in exchange for goods and services.
stable	The value is established and secure.
portable	It is convenient to carry around.
scarce	There is not enough to satisfy everyone's needs and wants.
divisible	It is easily divided into smaller parts.
durable	It will hold up under constant use.

Guarding Against Counterfeiting

The currency of the United States has undergone several changes in appearance since the first paper money was issued during the Revolutionary War. Recently, security features have been incorporated into the design to make it more secure against counterfeiting. **Counterfeiting** is illegally reproducing money for circulation. The **Secret Service** is the agency that investigates crimes involving the counterfeiting of United States money.

Security Features	Description
color-shifting ink	The numeral on the lower right corner changes color when the bill is tilted back and forth.
watermark	When the bill is held up to the light, another portrait of the person featured on the bill is visible.
security thread	A thread embedded in the bill glows when held under an ultraviolet light.
microprinting	The words "The United States of America" are printed so small they are hard to replicate.
fine-line printing patterns	Selected areas of the bill contain very thin lines incorporated in the design.

Name: _____ Date: _____

Assessment

Matching

_____ 1.   counterfeiting   a.   agency that investigates crimes of counterfeiting
_____ 2.   unit of accounting   b.   accepted in exchange for goods or services
_____ 3.   Secret Service   c.   can be saved for future purchases
_____ 4.   medium of exchange   d.   illegally reproducing money for circulation
_____ 5.   store of value   e.   can be used in the keeping of records

Fill in the Blank

1.   Recently, _____ features have been incorporated into the design
     of bills to make them more secure against _____.

2.   Money functions as a _____ of _____ for goods
     and services.

3.   People can _____ money for future needs and wants.

4.   On some United States paper money, the numeral on the lower right corner changes
     _____ when the bill is tilted back and forth.

5.   A thread _____ in the bill glows when held under an
     _____ light.

6.   The words "The _____ _____ of
     _____" are printed so small they are hard to replicate.

Constructed Response

Suppose the United States has decided that it must change its currency from coins and paper
money. Would rocks be an acceptable choice as a medium of exchange? Use information from
the Characteristics of Money chart to support your opinion.

_____

_____

_____

_____

_____

Historical Connection

Activity One

Primary Source:

<http://memory.loc.gov/ampage?collId=icufaw&fileName=bpc0004/icufawbpc0004browse.
   db&action=browse&recNum=0+title2>
   The First American West: The Ohio River Valley, 1750-1820. The Library of Congress.

Directions: Counterfeiting was a problem in colonial times. American colonies printed money
   in the form of bills of credit even though they were forbidden to do so by England. Students
   locate the primary source with this web address or do a search by keyword on the Library
   of Congress site using the exact words <u>indented bill</u>. Select *"The First American West...,"*
   and then *"This indented bill of five shillings...",* and then click on *"View Page Images"* to see
   both sides of the bill. As stated on the primary source, the punishment for counterfeiting
   was death. On July 5, 1865, the Secret Service was formed to stop counterfeiting. Over
   time, its duties have been expanded. Students research the Secret Service and create a
   list of its current duties and responsibilities.

Activity Two

Primary Source:

<http://historicaltextarchive.com/sections.php?op=viewarticle&artid=650>
   Mabry, Don J. *Currency Act, 1764.* 2007. The Historical Text Archive.

Directions: People living in the American colonies did not have sufficient currency to use for
   trading. Since the colonies were forbidden by England to print money, they printed bills
   of credit to use as money. The currency depreciated because bills of credit did not have
   a standard value, meaning that the redemption value varied. On September 1, 1764,
   Parliament passed the Currency Act. This act gave England control of the colonial currency
   system. Students examine the primary source and summarize the five provisions of the
   Currency Act.

Activity Three

Primary Source:

<http://memory.loc.gov/cgi-bin/query/r?ammem/mgw:@field(DOCID+@lit(lw010043))>
   "Horatio Sharpe to Cherokee Indians, 1756." *The George Washington Papers at the
   Library of Congress, 1741-1799.* The Library of Congress.

Directions: Wampum was once used as a medium of exchange. Wampum was beads made
   from clam shells and other types of shells strung together. Its value was derived from
   the beauty of the beads and the difficulty in making them. Purple wampum beads were
   worth twice as much as the white ones. Students examine the primary source to explore
   how wampum was also used to record or commemorate important events. By 1637, the
   Massachusetts Bay Colony declared wampum legal tender. They set an exchange rate for
   wampum: 6 white beads = 1 penny. Students look at newspaper
   advertisements for prices of food items. Using the above exchange
   rate, they convert the price of food items into wampum rates.

Knowledge Builder

Secret Service Agents

The Secret Service has many responsibilities. The main role of the agency is to investigate crimes involving counterfeiting. Secret Service agents rely on information from the public to apprehend counterfeiters. To avoid accepting counterfeited money, the public needs to be familiar with security features used in the design of paper money. The United States Secret Service web site provides current information on security features of bills and counterfeiting. Using research gleaned from this web site, students design an informational brochure on counterfeiting.

Designing Money

The paper money of the United States has many unique features. Symbols are often incorporated into the design of the bills. Supply several one-dollar bills for the class to examine. For security, place each bill in a sealed plastic bag. Students inspect the obverse and reverse sides of a one dollar bill for symbols. They research to find the official name and meaning for each symbol located on Federal Reserve notes. Using the research, students design a multimedia presentation explaining the symbolism featured on Federal Reserve notes.

Federal Reserve Note Investigation

Divide students into teams. Each team examines a $1, $2, $5, $10, and $20 bill to find the information needed to complete the Security Features table on page 22. Try to supply bills with the most current security features. For security, place each bill in a sealed plastic bag. Students use magnifying glasses to help locate microprinting and fine-line printing. An ultraviolet light is needed to discover the location and color of security threads.

Name: _____ Date: _____

Federal Reserve Note Investigation (Continued)

Security Features

Directions: Examine the security features on U.S. Federal Reserve notes and complete the table.

Bills	$1	$2	$5	$10	$20
Date of Issue					
Color of Security Thread					
Location of Security Thread					
Words on Security Thread					
Color of Shifting Ink					
Words Used in Microprinting					
Location of Microprinting					
Person Featured on Note					
Watermark	yes/no	yes/no	yes/no	yes/no	yes/no
Serial Number					

Teacher Resource Bank

National Standards Correlation:

NCEE Standard 11 (Role of Money): Money makes it easier to trade, borrow, save, invest, and compare value of goods and services.

NET Standard 5 (Technology Research Tools): Students use technology to locate, evaluate, and collect information from a variety of sources.

Bookshelf Resources:

Bailey, Gerry and Felicia Law. *Cowries, Coins, Credit: The History of Money.* Compass Point Books, 2006.

Cooper, Jason. *American Coins and Bills.* Rourke Publishing Group, 2002.

Rau, Dana Meachen. *Paper Money.* Weekly Reader Early Learning Library, 2005.

Seuling, Barbara. *Ancient Coins Were Shaped Like Hams: and Other Freaky Facts About Coins, Bills, and Counterfeiting.* Picture Window Books, 2008.

Online Resources:

<http://www.secretservice.gov/money_design_features.shtml>
"Design Features Which Vary on Genuine Currency." *Know Your Money.* 2006. United States Secret Service.

<http://www.frbsf.org/federalreserve/money/funfacts.html>
"Fun Facts About Money." *About the Fed.* Federal Reserve Bank of San Francisco.

<http://www.treas.gov/offices/domestic-finance/acd/if-you-suspect.shtml>
"If You Suspect a Counterfeit." *Advanced Counterfeit Deterrence.* United States Department of the Treasury.

<http://www.pbs.org/wgbh/nova/moolah/history.html>
Nova Online: Secrets of Making Money. August 2002. Public Broadcasting Service.

<http://www.ushistory.org/declaration/related/currencyact.htm>
Kindig, Thomas. "The Currency Act." *Related Information: Laws and Resolutions.* 2007. Independence Hall Association.

<http://www.coins.nd.edu/>
Jordan, Louis. *Coin and Currency Collections.* University of Notre Dame.

<http://www.frbatlanta.org/invoke_brochure.cfm?objectid=83FD4205-9AF0-11D5-898400508 BB89A83&method=display_body>
"Spotting Counterfeit Currency." *Dollars and Cents.* 7 Dec. 2006. Federal Reserve Bank of Atlanta.

Economics

What Is Economics?

Economics is the study of how things are bought and sold. When you go to the store and buy milk, you are participating in the local economy. When your parents buy a new house, they are participating in the national economy. And when you buy something made in China, you are participating in the global economy. To be a part of an economy, you must buy and sell goods or services.

Goods and services are the products that satisfy our needs and wants. **Goods** are any items that can be bought or sold. Some examples of goods are clothing, bicycles, breakfast cereals, and computers. A **service** is any action that one person or group does for another in exchange for payment. Some people who provide services include teachers, cooks, lawyers, bankers, comedians, and nurses.

Each region of the United States produces goods and services, depending on the available resources. A **resource** is anything used to produce goods and services. For example, Washington is one of the top-ranked states in apple production. Its soil, a natural resource, is suitable for growing apples. Similarly, West Virginia is a region rich in coal. **Production** is the process of changing raw materials into economic goods that can be used to satisfy the needs and wants of consumers.

Scarcity means we can never have all we want of every good and service. Desires and wants for goods and services are unlimited, while the resources needed to produce them are limited. Scarcity of resources includes money and time. Citizens, businesses, and governments make economic decisions based on the most effective use of their scarce resources. Countries rich in resources are able to better meet the needs and wants of their citizens.

Microeconomics vs. Macroeconomics

Microeconomics is the study of economic decisions made by consumers and producers that affect individuals in an economy. **Macroeconomics** is the study of economic decisions that affect the economy of a nation.

Microeconomics	Macroeconomics
A grocery store has a buy-one-get-one-free sale.	The Federal Reserve lowers interest rates.
A cell phone company offers a family rate plan.	Congress tackles Social Security issues.
A youth organization seeks to recruit volunteers.	The nation's unemployment reaches a 20-year low.
The local library extends its hours.	The United States' trade deficit widens with China.
The city passes a 3¢ gas tax.	OPEC raises the price per barrel of crude oil.

Name: _____ Date: _____

Assessment

Matching

_____ 1. macroeconomics   a. items that can be bought or sold

_____ 2. microeconomics   b. anything used to produce goods and services

_____ 3. resource   c. any action that one person or group does for another in exchange for payment

_____ 4. service   d. the study of economic decisions that affect the economy of a nation

_____ 5. goods   e. study of economic decisions made by consumers and producers that affect individuals in an economy

Fill in the Blank

1. Economics is the study of how things are _____ and

   _____.

2. Goods and services are the _____ that satisfy our needs and wants.

3. Some people who provide services include _____, _____,

   _____, _____, _____, and

   _____.

4. Production is the process of changing _____ materials into economic

   goods.

5. Scarcity of resources includes _____ and _____.

Constructed Response

In your own words, explain the statement, "Desires and wants for goods and services are unlimited, while resources needed to produce them are limited." Give examples and details to support your answer.

_____

_____

_____

_____

Historical Connection

Primary Source:
<http://memory.loc.gov/cgi-bin/query/r?ammem/rbpe:@field(DOCID+@lit(rbpe08801800))>
"At a convention of delegates…" *An American Time Capsule: Three Centuries of Broadsides and Other Printed Ephemera.* The Library of Congress.

Directions: Macroeconomics is the study of economic decisions that affect the whole economy of a nation. In 1779, delegates met at a convention in Exeter, New Hampshire. One of their concerns was how to support the credit of the Continental Currency. Students examine the primary source in order to answer the following Document-Based Questions (DBQs) on their own paper.

1. What was the reason given for setting the highest amount that could be charged for certain commodities?

2. According to the resolves, the highest price that could be charged for cider was 6 British pounds (£) per "barrel." Using a currency converter calculator, what does this amount equal in U.S. currency today?

3. Summarize the four reasons given to encourage people to comply with the resolves.

Knowledge Builder

Goods and Services

Anything people buy and sell can be classified as goods or services. Using the local newspaper or telephone book, students identify businesses that offer goods and services. Using the research, students design an informational poster about businesses offering services and businesses offering goods.

Microeconomics vs. Macroeconomics

Divide a bulletin board into two sections with one side titled MICROECONOMICS and the other MACROECONOMICS. Students collect articles on economic topics from magazines, newspapers, or online sources. After discussing an article, students classify it as a microeconomic or macroeconomic issue. Then display the article under the correct heading.

Teacher Resource Bank

National Standards Correlation:

NCEE Standard 1 (Scarcity): Productive resources are limited. Therefore, people cannot have all the goods and services they want; as a result, they must choose some things and give up others.

NET Standard 5 (Technology Research Tools): Students use technology to locate, evaluate, and collect information from a variety of sources.

Bookshelf Resources:

Adil, Janeen R. *Goods and Services.* Capstone Press, 2006.

Cefrey, Holly. *The Interstate Commerce Act: The Government Takes Control of Trade Between States.* Rosen Central Primary Source, 2004.

Goldberg, Jan. *The Department of Commerce.* Rosen Classroom, 2005.

Ridgway, Tom. *The Young Zillionaire's Guide to Buying Goods and Services.* Rosen Publishing Group, 2000.

Online Resources:

<http://usinfo.state.gov/products/pubs/economy-in-brief/page2.html>
    "Goods and Services." *USA Economy in Brief.* U.S. Department of State.

<http://eh.net/hmit/>
    "How Much is That?" *EH.Net.* Economic History Services.

<http://usinfo.state.gov/products/pubs/economy-in-brief/page8.html>
    "Macroeconomic Policy." *USA Economy in Brief.* U.S. Department of State.

<http://www.fte.org/teachers/programs/efl/lessons/lesson1.htm>
    "Scarcity and Choice." *Economics for Leaders.* Foundation for Teaching Economics.

<http://www.economicadventure.org/teachers/glossary_econ.cfm>
    "Terms and Theory." *Especially for Teachers.* New England Economic Adventure.

<http://www.investopedia.com/ask/answers/110.asp>
    "What's the difference between macroeconomics and microeconomics?"
    Frequently Asked Questions. 2007. Investopedia.

Factors of Production

Types of Resources

Individuals, families, businesses, and the government make economic decisions concerning the use of a nation's resources. These resources are typically categorized into four groups called **factors of production**: land, labor, capital, and entrepreneurship.

Factors of Production

Land is the environmental resource. It includes all natural resources: land (including anything that grows on or below the soil), water, air, and wildlife. Some natural resources are plentiful, while others are scarce. Resources are classified as renewable and nonrenewable. A renewable resource is one that can be replaced, either naturally or by man. A nonrenewable resource is one that cannot be replaced in a timely manner or at all by nature or by man. Payment for the use of land is called **rent**.

Labor is the mental and physical efforts of people applied to the production of goods and services. Labor is an important element of production. Workers labor to make goods and provide services. Payment for labor is called **wages**. In 1913, the Department of Labor was established to enforce laws created to protect workers against unfair labor practices by businesses.

Capital is the money, buildings, and machinery and equipment used to produce goods and services. Payment for investing capital is called **interest**. **Capitalism** is an economic system used by many nations, including the United States. Under this system, private individuals and corporations own the capital used to produce goods and services.

Entrepreneurship is the risk-taking resource. Entrepreneurs are people who combine labor, land, and capital resources to start businesses. Not every business is successful; sometimes they fail. Payment for risk-taking or entrepreneurship is called **profit**. An important characteristic of capitalism is **free enterprise**: individuals own businesses to make a profit. The **profit motive**, the possibility of making money, is the main reason people take the risk of starting a business. Competition between businesses allows consumers to purchase the best quality product at the lowest price.

Name: _____ Date: _____

Assessment

Matching

_____ 1. entrepreneurship   a. the environmental resources
_____ 2. free enterprise   b. the risk-taking resource
_____ 3. capital   c. mental and physical efforts of people applied to the
                                         production of goods and services
_____ 4. labor   d. individuals own businesses to make a profit
_____ 5. land   e. money, buildings, machinery and equipment used to
                                         produce goods and services

Fill in the Blank

1. Resources are typically categorized into four groups called _____

   _____ _____: land, labor, capital, and entrepreneurship.

2. Payment for the use of land is called _____.

3. Payment for labor is called _____.

4. _____ is an economic system used by many nations, including the

   United States.

5. Payment for risk-taking or entrepreneurship is called _____.

Constructed Response

A renewable resource is one that can be replaced, either naturally or by man. A nonrenewable resource is one that cannot be replaced in a timely manner or at all by nature or by man. Complete the table by listing resources under the correct heading.

Renewable Resources	Nonrenewable Resources
Example: trees	Example: gold

Historical Connection

Activity One

Primary Source:
<http://memory.loc.gov/cgi-bin/query/r?ammem/faw:@field(DOCID+icufawcmf0014)>
"Letter from Barthelemi Tardiveau to St. John de Crevecour." *The First American West: The Ohio River Valley, 1750-1820.* The Library of Congress.

 **Directions:** The four factors of production are land, labor, capital, and entrepreneurship. On August 25, 1789, Barthelemi Tardiveau wrote a letter about a trip that he had taken into "Cumberland country." He writes St. John de Crevecour about his interest in the cotton market that he viewed during his trip. Students examine the primary source, identifying examples of the four factors of production mentioned in Tardiveau's letter.

Activity Two

Primary Source:
<http://memory.loc.gov/cgi-bin/query/b?ammem/fsaall:LC-USE613-D-002381:collection=fsa>
America from the Great Depression to World War II: Black-and-White Photographs from the FSA-OWI, 1935-1945. 15 Dec. 1995. The Library of Congress.

Directions: During World War II, the government imposed mandatory rationing on many commodities. In 1942, sugar began to be rationed in the United States. Students locate the primary source web link. When the web page opens, select the images labeled LC-USE613-D-002383 and LC-USE613-D-002384. These images are titled, "Sugar rationing. Instructions on the use of the war ration book." Students read through the instructions for rationing. Then they imagine that pencils are being rationed in their classroom. As a class, students create instructions for the rationing of pencils.

Knowledge Builder

Product Map

Product maps show the locations and types of resources found in a geographic area. Students create a product map identifying and locating the natural resources available in their state.

Natural Resources

Resources are necessary for businesses to manufacture goods and provide services. Students compile a list of all the resources used to produce their favorite snacks or breakfast cereals. Using a graphic organizer, they identify each resource as one of the factors of production: land, labor, capital, and entrepreneurship.

Teacher Resource Bank

National Standards Correlation:

NCEE Standard 1 (Scarcity): Productive resources are limited. Therefore, people can not have all the goods and services they want; as a result, they must choose some things and give up others.

NET Standard 5 (Technology Research Tools): Students use technology to locate, evaluate, and collect information from a variety of sources.

Bookshelf Resources:

Emert, Phyllis ed. *World War II: On the Homefront.* Discovery Enterprises, 1996.

Gilman, Laura Anne. *Economics: How Economics Works.* Lerner Publications, 2006.

Poggio, Pier Paolo and Carlo Simoni. *The Industrial Revolution, 1800–1850.* Chelsea House Publications, 2002.

Tillema, Juliana O. *The Young Zillionaire's Guide to Producing Goods and Services.* Rosen Publishing Group, 2000.

Williams, Brenda. *The Home Front: World at War—World War II.* Heinemann Library, 2006.

Online Resources:

<http://usinfo.state.gov/products/pubs/economy-in-brief/page5.html>
   "Businesses Large and Small." *USA Economy in Brief.* U.S. Department of State.

<http://www.econedlink.org/lessons/index.cfm>
   "Online Lessons." *EconEdLink.* National Council on Economic Education.

<http://library.duke.edu/digitalcollections/catalog/hfc/>
   Ration Coupons on the Home Front, 1942-1945. 2006. Duke University Libraries.

<http://www.bbc.co.uk/history/ww2children/ration/ration_intro.shtml>
   "Rationing Challenge." *Children of World War 2.* BBC.

<http://usinfo.state.gov/products/pubs/economy-in-brief/page6.html>
   "Workers and Productivity." *USA Economy in Brief.* U.S. Department of State.

Supply and Demand

Supply and Demand

The economy of the United States is based on providing consumers with the goods and services they need and want. **Consumers** are people who buy and use goods and services. **Producers** are the people and businesses that provide these goods and services for the consumers. The goods and services made available to consumers are determined by **supply and demand**.

Supply is the number of items ready for sale. **Demand** is the number of items consumers want to purchase. If the supply of an item is greater than its demand by consumers, then there is a surplus of that item. A **surplus** causes the price of the item to decrease. When consumers' demand for the item is greater than the supply, this results in a scarcity. **Scarcity** causes the price of the item to increase.

Law of Supply and Demand
1. The price of an item will go down if the supply increases or the demand for that item decreases.
2. The price of an item will go up if the supply decreases or the demand for that item increases.

Early Examples of Supply and Demand

Jamestown Colony prospered from tobacco production. Tobacco sold for very high prices in England due to the high demand for the product. This encouraged settlers to plant more tobacco to take advantage of the high prices.

In 1849, gold was discovered in California. People from all over the world rushed to California to get rich in the gold fields. With limited supplies of goods and services available to the prospectors, the prices of items such as food, lodging, and supplies skyrocketed.

After the Civil War, small farms operated by sharecroppers and tenant farmers replaced the large plantations. With few resources, the farmers depended on credit to purchase the goods and services they needed. To repay their debts, farmers grew cotton as a cash crop. Eventually, more cotton was produced than could be sold, and the price of cotton fell drastically.

Today

The cost of energy is a concern for consumers. One form of energy is fossil fuels. Oil is a fossil fuel that is a nonrenewable resource. There is a limited supply available. As other nations build more factories, drive more cars, and buy more computers, the rising demand for oil causes an increase in oil prices. Future demand by individuals, businesses, and nations for fossil fuels will continue to cause increases in the price of fossil fuels, unless the demand can be satisfied by alternative energy sources.

Name: _____ Date: _____

Assessment

Matching

_____ 1. demand   a. supply is greater than demand

_____ 2. supply   b. number of items wanted for purchase

_____ 3. consumers   c. when demand is greater than supply

_____ 4. surplus   d. the people and businesses that provide goods and
                                services

_____ 5. producers   e. number of items ready for sale

_____ 6. scarcity   f. people who buy and use goods and services

Fill in the Blank

1. Scarcity causes the price of the item to _____.

2. Jamestown Colony prospered from _____ production.

3. With limited supplies of goods and services available to the prospectors during the Gold

    Rush, the prices for food, lodging, and supplies _____.

4. Oil, a fossil fuel, is a _____ resource.

Constructed Response

Why does the price of a coat increase in the winter and decrease in the summer? Use the Law of Supply and Demand to explain your answer.

_____

_____

_____

_____

_____

_____

_____

_____

Historical Connection

Primary Source:

<http://memory.loc.gov/cgi-bin/query/r?ammem/calbk:@field%28DOCID+@lit%28calbk067 div35%29%29:>

"Sacramento City, November 25, 1849." *A Yankee trader in the gold rush; the letters of Franklin A. Buck.* The Library of Congress.

Directions: In 1848, James Wilson Marshall discovered gold at Sutter's Mill. As news spread, thousands rushed to California to seek their fortune in the gold fields. With a limited supply of goods and services available to prospectors, prices skyrocketed. Students examine Franklin A. Buck's letter to his sister. Using the information found in the letter, students construct mathematical word problems to find the profits made from the sale of flour.

Knowledge Builder

Class Auction

Auctions are effective in demonstrating the connection between supply and demand and the price of goods. Over a period of days, issue tickets to students for turning in assignments on time, performing acts of kindness, following classroom rules, or being polite. Collect items to auction, such as books, markers, posters, or donations from local businesses. Schedule an "inspection period" before the actual auction. To demonstrate the effect scarcity has on the price of items, be sure to limit the supply of the most desired items. Offer large quantities of less desirable items. The day of the auction, explain the auction process to students.

- The current item for bid is held up for everyone to see.
- Students raise their hand to signify a bid on an item.
- The highest bid wins the item.
- Tickets are exchanged for the item won in the bidding.

After the auction, discuss the effect supply and demand had on the final price of the item.

Advertising and Consumers

The purpose of advertising is to sell a product. In order to make informed decisions, consumers need to recognize advertising techniques and strategies. Sometimes, slogans or jingles are used to catch the consumer's attention. Persuasive advertising techniques such as bandwagon, testimonial, and repetition are also used to promote products. Students research and define advertising techniques. Using magazines, they collect examples of each technique. Also, students create a list of advertising jingles and slogans used by businesses. Using similar techniques, students design an advertising campaign for a product they use every day.

Teacher Resource Bank

National Standards Correlation:

NCEE Standard 5 (Gain From Trade): Voluntary exchange occurs only when all participating parties expect to gain. This is true for trade among individuals or organizations within a nation, and usually among individuals or organizations in different nations.

NET Standard 5 (Technology Research Tools): Students use technology to locate, evaluate, and collect information from a variety of sources.

Bookshelf Resources:

Adil, Janeen R. *Scarcity.* Capstone Press, 2006.

Adil, Janeen R. *Supply and Demand.* Capstone Press, 2006.

Gilman, Laura Anne. *Economics: How Economics Works.* Lerner Publications, 2005.

Seidman, David. *The Young Zillionaire's Guide to Supply and Demand.* Rosen Publishing Group, 2000.

Online Resources:

<http://usinfo.state.gov/products/pubs/oecon/>
 Conte, Christopher, and Albert R. Karr. *An Outline of the U.S. Economy.* U.S. Department of State.

<http://www.investopedia.com/university/economics/economics3.asp>
 "Demand and Supply." *Economics Basics.* 2008. Investopedia.

<http://www.econedlink.org/lessons/index.cfm?lesson=EM369>
 Lemon Squeeze—The Lemonade Stand. National Council on Economic Education.

<http://usinfo.state.gov/products/pubs/economy-in-brief/page8.html>
 "Macroeconomic Policy." *USA Economy in Brief.* U.S. Department of State.

<http://www.socialstudiesforkids.com/articles/economics/supplyanddemand1.htm>
 White, David. *Supply and Demand: Basic Economics.* 2007. Social Studies for Kids.

Opportunity Cost and Trade-offs

Economic Decisions

When making economic decisions, limited resources force individuals, businesses, and nations to make trade-offs. **Trade-offs** result in giving up something of value to get what is most wanted. Sometimes the choice can involve the resource of time, for example, choosing to volunteer at an animal shelter instead of going with friends to the local mall. At other times, the choice may involve money—buy the newest music CD or save for a cell phone?

Opportunity Cost

Every time an economic decision is made, there is the risk of not selecting the best choice. The **opportunity cost** of a decision is what is given up when the alternative choice is not selected. For example, the opportunity cost of deciding to spend one hour studying for a math test is the lost opportunity to spend time with friends. The risk is whether the extra time studying will result in a higher test score.

In business, entrepreneurs make economic decisions hoping the payoff will be profits. The opportunity cost of making a profit includes the entrepreneur limiting the investment of money in advertising, remodeling, or higher wages for workers.

In government, economic decisions are made concerning how to best provide citizens with goods and services they are not able to provide for themselves. The opportunity cost of decisions includes sacrificing funding to other budget items. For example, fully funding national defense might result in a decrease in funding for services such as transportation or education.

Steps In The Economic Decision-Making Process

Economic decision: How to spend Saturday afternoon?			
Step One:	List criteria for making the decision. • Example—earning money; outdoor activity		
Step Two:	List all the choices to consider. • Example—skateboarding with friends; going to the movies; earning money mowing lawns		
Step Three:	Consider the advantages and disadvantages of each choice, then rank.		
Choice	Rank	Advantage	Disadvantage
Skateboarding with friends	2	outdoor activity, not spending money	not earning money
Going to the movies	3	indoor activity	spending money, not earning money
Earning money mowing lawns	1	outdoor activity	earning money
Step Four:	Identify the choice and the opportunity cost of the decision. • Example—The choice is earning money by mowing the lawn. The opportunity cost of the decision is not skateboarding with friends, since it is the next-highest-ranked alternative.		

Name: _____ Date: _____

Assessment

Fill in the Blank

1. Limited resources force individuals, businesses, and nations to make

   _____.

2. _____ result in giving up something of value to get what is wanted

   most.

3. The _____ _____ of a decision is what is given up

   when the alternative choice is not selected.

4. In business, _____ make economic decisions.

5. The opportunity costs of making a profit include the entrepreneur limiting the investment of

   money in _____, _____, or _____.

Constructed Response

You have an economic decision to make. You have $50.00 to spend. Should you purchase sports equipment to use at home, a ticket to attend a professional sporting event, or sports memorabilia for your football collection?

Steps In The Economic Decision-Making Process

Economic decision:			
Step One:	List criteria for making the decision.		
Step Two:	List all the choices to consider.		
Step Three:	Consider the advantages and disadvantages of each choice, then rank.		

Choice	Rank	Advantage	Disadvantage

Step Four:	Identify the choice and the opportunity cost of the decision.

Historical Connection

Primary Sources:

<http://scriptorium.lib.duke.edu/adaccess/TV/TV04/TV0492-72dpi.jpeg>
> DuMont. "For Christmas this Year—What Finer Gift?" *Ad*Access.* 1999. Duke University Libraries.

<http://scriptorium.lib.duke.edu/adaccess/R/R01/R0102-72dpi.jpeg>
> General Electric. "Musaphonic." *Ad*Access.* 1999. Duke University Libraries.

Directions: Consumers are always making choices. Opportunity cost and trade-offs have to be considered. Students pretend that it is Christmas time, and they have saved $200 to buy a gift for the family. Their choices are a phonograph/radio that costs $50 or a television that costs $125. Students examine the primary sources for product information. Using the steps in the economic decision-making process, students justify their gift selection.

Knowledge Builder

Product Information

The more a consumer knows about a product, the easier it is to make a wise choice. Federal and state laws require manufacturers to attach certain information to the product or packaging. Evaluating product information often reveals that one product is a better choice for the consumer. Students visit a local store or supermarket. Using information found on labels or packaging, they compare different brands of the same type of product. Students use a graphic organizer to record their information.

Quality Check

It is important for a consumer to find out about the quality of a product before purchasing the item. For example, *Good Housekeeping* magazine issues a Seal of Approval to select products. Students explore the *Good Housekeeping* web site (see *Online Resources*) to answer the questions listed below on their own paper.

Questions:

1. What year was the *Good Housekeeping* Seal instituted?

2. What is the *Good Housekeeping* Consumer's Policy?

3. What are the names of five products that carry the Seal?

Teacher Resource Bank

National Standards Correlation:
NCEE Standard 11 (Role of Money): Money makes it easier to trade, borrow, save, invest, and compare the value of goods and services.

NET Standard 5 (Technology Research Tools): Students use technology to locate, evaluate, and collect information from a variety of sources.

Bookshelf Resources:
Bodnar, Janet. *Mom, Can I Have That?* Kiplinger Books, 1996.

Donovan, Sandy. *Budgeting.* Lerner Publications, 2005.

Heckman, Philip. *Saving Money.* Lerner Publications, 2005.

Lermitte, Paul W. *Making Allowances: Dollars and Sense.* McGraw-Hill, 2002.

Mayr, Diane. *The Everything Kids' Money Book: From Saving to Spending to Investing—Learn All About Money!* Adams Media, 2000.

Online Resources:
<http://ecedweb.unomaha.edu/lessons/M&M6-8.pdf>
"Lesson Four: M & M Interesting." *Personal Finance Economics, 6-8: Money in the Middle.* National Council on Economic Education.

<http://pbskids.org/itsmylife/money/managing/index.html>
"Managing Money: Spending and Saving." *It's My Life.* 2005. PBSKids.

<http://www.netmba.com/econ/micro/cost/opportunity/>
Opportunity Cost. NetMBA.com.

<http://www.econedlink.org/lessons/index.cfm?page=teacher&lesson=EM51>
"The Opportunity Cost of a Lifetime." *Economics.* 2007. National Council on Economic Education.

<http://googolplex.cuna.org/00001A/ajsmall/index.html>
"Today's Specials." *AJ's Mall.* Googolplex: The Credit Union Guide for Student Money Makers.

<http://www.goodhousekeepingseal.com/r5/display.asp?file=seal.asp>
"What's Behind the Good Housekeeping Seal?" *Good Housekeeping Seal Directory.* 2008. The Hearst Corporation.

Economic Systems

Three Basic Economic Questions

The needs and wants of individuals, families, businesses, and nations for goods and services are unlimited. The resources to satisfy these needs and wants are limited; therefore, every nation is faced with answering these questions.

- What goods and services will be produced?
- Who will be responsible for producing the goods and services?
- How will the goods and services be distributed to consumers?

There is no absolute correct way of allocating scarce resources. A particular method might prove to be ideal in one situation but less satisfactory in other situations. Each nation must select an economic system to allocate resources. There are three basic economic systems: **traditional**, **command**, and **market**.

Methods of Allocation

In a **traditional economic system**, economic decisions are based on a society's customs, culture, and way of life. Hunting, farming, gathering, and making things by hand are the methods used to meet the people's needs under this system. Tradition assumes that things do not change, and if it worked well in the past, it will work as well in the future.

In a **command economic system**, the government makes economic decisions. The government owns most of the industries. In a command economy, it is important for producers to meet the government's assigned production **quotas**, which are the amounts of goods and services to produce. Prices are set by the government and do not change according to supply and demand.

The **market economic system** is the method used in the United States. In our "free market system," consumers and producers decide what to produce, how much to produce, and the worth of goods and services. Entrepreneurs or business owners seeing an opportunity for profits will produce and market goods or services. If entrepreneurs do a good job in anticipating the desires of the consumers, then they will make profits. If the entrepreneurs do a poor job, there will be a loss in profit.

Name: _____ Date: _____

Assessment

Matching

_____ 1. market economic system
_____ 2. quotas
_____ 3. entrepreneurs
_____ 4. traditional economic system
_____ 5. command economic system

a. assigned amounts of goods and services to be produced

b. consumers and producers decide what to produce, how much to produce, and the worth of goods and services

c. decisions are made according to customs, culture, and way of life

d. business owners

e. government makes economic decisions

Fill in the Blank

1. The market economic system is the method used in the _____ _____.

2. Entrepreneurs or business owners seeing an opportunity for _____ will produce and market a good or service.

3. In a traditional economic system, economic decisions are made according to _____.

4. In a command economy, it is important for producers to meet their government-assigned production _____.

Constructed Response

Complete the following chart.

Economic System	Advantages	Disadvantages
Market		
Traditional		
Command		

Historical Connection

Primary Source:
<http://www.nytimes.com/learning/general/onthisday/bday/0708.html>
    "Financier's Fortune in Oil Amassed in Industrial Era of 'Rugged Individualism.'" *On This Day.* 2007. The New York Times Company.

Directions: John D. Rockefeller was an entrepreneur, industrialist, and a philanthropist. Students examine the primary source, Rockefeller's obituary, to understand the contributions he made to American industry. Students research the life of other American entrepreneurs, such as Andrew Carnegie, J. P. Morgan, Henry Ford, Madam C. J. Walker, Ray Kroc, Walt Disney, Sam Walton, and Oprah Winfrey. Using their research, students create a multimedia presentation. The focus of the presentation should be on the financial decisions made by the entrepreneurs and the impact these decisions had on the U.S. economy.

Knowledge Builder

World Map Economy

There are three basic economic systems: traditional, command, and market. On their own paper, students construct a graphic organizer to identify the type of economic system used by each country listed below.

Country
United States of America
China
Cuba
Russia
Norway
Cameroon
Honduras
Japan
India
East Timor
Ethiopia
Australia
Saudi Arabia
France
North Korea

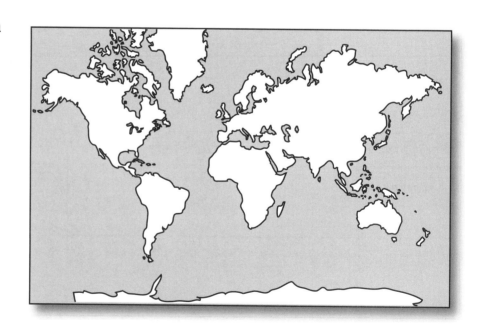

Teacher Resource Bank

National Standards Correlation:

NCEE Standard 3 (Allocation of Goods and Services): Different methods can be used to allocate goods and services. People acting individually or collectively through government must choose which method to use to allocate different kinds of goods and services.

NET Standard 5 (Technology Research Tools): Students use technology to locate, evaluate, and collect information from a variety of sources.

Bookshelf Resources:

Downing, David. *Capitalism.* Heinemann Library, 2008.

Downing, David. *Communism.* Heinemann Library, 2003.

Heilbroner, Robert L. and Lester C. Thurow. *Economics Explained: Everything You Need to Know About How the Economy Works and Where It's Going.* 4th ed. Simon & Schuster, 1998.

Lobb, Nancy. *16 Extraordinary American Entrepreneurs.* J. Weston Walch, 1998.

Tames, Richard. *Dictatorship.* Heinemann Library, 2003.

Online Resources:

<http://www.econedlink.org/lessons/index.cfm?page=teacher&lesson=EM322>
   "Comparative Economic Systems." *EconEdLink.* 2007. National Council on Economic Education.

<http://www.socialstudieshelp.com/Economic_Systems.htm>
   "Comparative Economic Systems." *Economics.* 2001-2006. The Social Studies Help Center.

<http://usinfo.state.gov/products/pubs/oecon/>
   Conte, Christopher, and Albert R. Karr. *An Outline of the U.S. Economy.* U.S. Department of State.

<http://www.entre-ed.org/_teach/econ-ed.htm>
   "Economics: The Foundation of Entrepreneurship." Consortium for Entrepreneurship Education.

<http://usinfo.state.gov/products/pubs/market/homepage.htm>
   Watts, Michael. *What is a Market Economy?* 1998. U.S. Department of State.

Organization of Business

How a business is organized depends on the size, purpose, and number of owners. People who combine the resources of land, labor, and/or capital in order to start businesses are called **entrepreneurs**. They are willing to take the risk of organizing and operating a new business venture in the hopes of making a profit. Some famous entrepreneurs include John D. Rockefeller, Andrew Carnegie, Henry Ford, Madam C. J. Walker, and Sam Walton.

Businesses may be operated as sole proprietorships, partnerships, or corporations. Each type of business organization has its advantages and disadvantages.

Types of Business Organization	Advantages	Disadvantages
Sole proprietorship: a business owned by one person.	• It is relatively easy to start a small business. The owners make all the business decisions: what to produce or sell, how much to charge customers, and what hours to work. • Owners receive all the profits if the business is successful.	• Owners provide all the capital to start and operate the business. • Owners are responsible to pay all the bills, hire all the employees, and usually must work long hours. • If the business fails, owners are responsible for all financial losses.
Partnership: two or more individuals combine to form a business	• Partners combine their resources, making it easier to get financing. • Partners share the work-load and duties. • If the business fails, owners share responsibility for financial losses.	• Partners may be involved in disagreements about the operation of the business. • If a partner makes a mistake or is dishonest, the business may be in jeopardy.
Corporation: a large business with many owners	• It is easier to finance growth because a corporation can sell stocks and bonds. • There is a limited financial **liability**, or responsibility, because stockholders can only lose their investment. • Corporations have the capital to hire people who are skilled in business management.	• There are extensive government regulations. • It may be harder to reach agreements between owners.

Name: _____ Date: _____

Assessment

Matching

_____ 1. partnership

_____ 2. corporation

_____ 3. sole proprietorship

_____ 4. liability

_____ 5. entrepreneur

a. large business with many owners

b. a business owned by one person

c. two or more individuals combine to form a business

d. responsibility

e. person who starts a business

Fill in the Blank

1. How a business is organized depends on the _____, purpose, and number of _____.

2. Some famous entrepreneurs include John D. Rockefeller, _____, _____, Henry Ford, Madam C. J. Walker, and _____ _____.

3. In a sole proprietorship, the _____ provides all the capital to start and operate the business.

4. In a _____, partners share the workload and duties.

5. Corporations have the _____ to hire people who are skilled in business management.

Constructed Response

Most businesses in the United States are sole proprietorships. Explain why an entrepreneur might start a new business as a sole proprietorship. Give specific examples and details to support your answer.

_____

_____

_____

_____

Historical Connection

Primary Source:
<http://scriptorium.lib.duke.edu/eaa/ephemera/A03/A0335/A0335-72dpi.html>
   "Hershey's Sweet Milk Chocolate." *Emergence of Advertising in America.* Duke University.

<www.mikescandywrappers.com/hersheys0902.html>
   "Hershey's Chocolate Bar." *Mike's Candy Wrappers.* 2007.

Directions: Milton S. Hershey was an inventor and entrepreneur. After serving an apprenticeship in candy making, he returned to Pennsylvania to start his own business, the Lancaster Caramel Company. It was a successful business, but Hershey sold it in 1900 so he could concentrate on chocolate candy making. Students examine the primary source, a 1900s Hershey's Sweet Milk Chocolate bar wrapper. Today, the Hershey Company still produces this brand of milk chocolate candy bar. Using a graphic organizer, students compare and contrast the information and design of the historical candy bar wrapper to the current wrapper. They then design a new wrapper for the chocolate bar.

Knowledge Builder

Classifying Companies

Each year the top 500 companies, based on revenue, are named to the prestigious *Fortune* 500 list. Students research one of the companies on the list. Using their research, they design an informational pamphlet about the company. Students should include pertinent facts in their pamphlets, such as the company's history, goals, products, number of employees, and profits.

Explore the Community

Students select a business in their community to research. Using their research, they design a visual aid to be used with an oral presentation featuring the business. Students should include information concerning:
- Type of business: sole proprietorship, partnership, and corporation
- History of the business
- Goods or services provided or produced
- Number of employees

Philanthropy

Successful entrepreneurs often become philanthropists. They use their wealth to support charitable causes. Students use the web site below to identify five famous philanthropists to research. Using the information, students create a graphic organizer identifying the philanthropist, their philanthropic activities, and the impact those activities had on the public.

<http://foundationcenter.org/focus/youth/kids_teens/youth_celebrity.html#famous>
   "Famous and Celebrity Philanthropists." *Youth in Philanthropy.* Foundation Center.

Teacher Resource Bank

National Standards Correlation:

NCEE Standard 14 (Profit and the Entrepreneur): Entrepreneurs are people who take the risks of organizing productive resources to make goods and services. Profit is an important incentive that leads entrepreneurs to accept the risks of business failure.

NET Standard 5 (Technology Research Tools): Students use technology to locate, evaluate, and collect information from a variety of sources.

Bookshelf Resources:

Bochner, Arthur and Rose Bochner. *The New Totally Awesome Business Book for Kids! Revised and Updated Third Edition.* Newmarket Press, 2007.

Clements, Andrew. *Lunch Money.* Simon & Schuster, 2005.

Giesecke, Ernestine. *Be Your Own Boss: Small Businesses.* Heinemann Library, 2003.

Murphy, Patricia J. *Earning Money.* Lerner Publications, 2005.

Rancic, Bill. *Beyond the Lemonade Stand: Starting Small to Make it Big!* Razorbill, 2005.

Online Resources:

<http://titan.ja.org/>
   JA Titan. 2006. Junior Achievement Worldwide.

<http://www.mindyourownbiz.org/default.shtml>
   Mind Your Own Business. 2008. U.S. Small Business Administration and Junior Achievement Worldwide.

<http://www.moneyopolis.org/new/home.asp>
   Moneyopolis: Where Money Sense Rules. 2003. Ernst & Young LLP.

<http://www.themint.org>
   The Mint: It Makes Perfect Cents. 2007. Northwestern Mutual.

The Business Cycle

The Business Cycle

"Good times" and "hard times" are phrases often used to describe the ups and downs in the U.S. economy. When the economy is growing or expanding, businesses increase production, work is plentiful, and people have money to spend. This **expansion**, or economic growth, leads to a time of financial prosperity. However, this period of expansion will not last forever because competition for goods and services causes **inflation**, or the increase, in prices. People are forced to pay more for goods and services, so they are able to buy less. When the economy finally slows down, people spend less money, companies cut back on production, and workers are laid off. Some businesses may fail or close. The economy then enters a **recession**, or a decline in business activity. A recession that continues for too long can become a **depression**. Eventually, the economy will pick up, and the cycle begins again. This continuous sequence of ups and downs in the economy is called the **business cycle**.

Examples From U.S. History

By 1920, World War I had ended, and the U.S. economy was booming. New products, buying on credit, and the use of electricity to power factories and homes kept businesses producing in record amounts. Even though President Calvin Coolidge encouraged thrift, it was a time of great prosperity. New inventions promised a bright future for all Americans. In the fall of 1929, the "good times" came to a sudden and screeching halt. The economic prosperity of the 1920s ended with the crash of the stock market. Within days, banks failed and businesses closed. Millions of people lost their jobs, homes, and life savings. President Hoover was blamed as poverty spread throughout the United States. Soup kitchens were set up to feed millions of hungry and homeless people. The country plunged into what is known as the Great Depression. Eventually, the programs of President Franklin D. Roosevelt's administration were instrumental in bringing about the economic recovery. The entry of the United States into World War II finally caused the economy to grow and prosper once again.

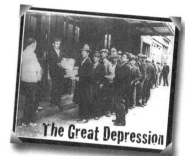
The Great Depression

Controlling the Economy

Today, the government continuously monitors and regulates the economy with its fiscal and monetary policies. When the economy is expanding, the government tries to slow down spending by people and businesses. To do this, they might raise interest rates and cut government spending. To combat inflation, people are encouraged to spend less and save more while businesses are encouraged to produce more to decrease prices. During a recession or depression, the government tries to increase the amount of money in the economy so people and businesses have more to spend. They might cut taxes, lower interest rates, or increase government spending on public works to keep companies and businesses producing and workers employed.

Name: _____   Date: _____

Assessment

Matching

_____ 1. business cycle   a. increase in prices

_____ 2. recession   b. recession that continues for too long

_____ 3. depression   c. decline in business activity

_____ 4. inflation   d. economic growth

_____ 5. expansion   e. the continuous sequence of ups and downs in the
                                    economy

Fill in the Blank

1. When the economy is _____ or _____, businesses

   increase production, work is plentiful, and people have money to spend.

2. Competition for goods and services causes _____.

3. By 1920, World War I had ended, and the U.S. economy was _____.

4. The economic prosperity of the 1920s ended with the crash of the _____

   _____.

5. Today, the government continuously _____ and _____

   the economy with its fiscal and monetary policies.

Constructed Response

Explain how inflation can affect your spending power. Give specific examples and details to
support your answer.

_____

_____

_____

_____

_____

_____

Historical Connection

Activity One

Primary Source:
<http://memory.loc.gov/cgi-bin/ampage?collId=amrlgs&fileName=gh1page.db&recNum=100>
  "*Good Housekeeping* selected issue from 1926." *Prosperity and Thrift: The Coolidge Era and the Consumer Economy, 1921-1929.* The Library of Congress.

Directions: During the Roaring Twenties, new products and inventions changed the way Americans lived. On the web site, students click "Next Image" several times to view various ads. Students examine the primary source to identify advertising strategies used to promote these consumer products. They select one item, such as the telephone, vacuum cleaner, refrigerator, washing machine, radio, or automobile, developed or improved during this decade. Using their research, students create a magazine cover for *Good Housekeeping* illustrating the role new technology played in shaping the booming economy of the 1920s.

Activity Two

Primary Source:
<http://newdeal.feri.org/eleanor/1h1136.htm>
  "Miss L. H., Gravette, Ark." *Dear Mrs. Roosevelt.* The New Deal Network.

Directions: During the first term of FDR's presidency, First Lady Eleanor Roosevelt supported New Deal programs that brought relief to young people. Two of these programs were the National Youth Administration and lunch programs in schools. Students research one of the New Deal programs that directly benefited youth. Students read examples, located in the primary source, of letters Mrs. Roosevelt received from children. Students select one of the letters and write a paragraph explaining how a New Deal program could help solve the problem described in the letter.

Knowledge Builder

1920s/1930s Compare and Contrast

Students work together to create a classroom bulletin board that compares and contrasts the lives of Americans during the 1920s and 1930s. Divide a bulletin board into two sections with one side titled **1920s** and the other **1930s**. Students collect photographs and quotations about these decades from the Internet. They arrange the information to form two separate collages. Using the board, students review how changes in the economy can affect the standard of living.

Teacher Resource Bank

National Standards Correlation:
<u>NCEE Standard 18 (Macroeconomy-Income/Employment, Prices)</u>: A nation's overall levels of income, employment, and prices are determined by the interaction of spending and production decisions made by all households, firms, government agencies, and others in the economy.

<u>NET Standard 5 (Technology Research Tools)</u>: Students use technology to locate, evaluate, and collect information from a variety of sources.

Bookshelf Resources:
Gilman, Laura Anne. *Economics.* Lerner Publications, 2006.

Landau, Elaine. *The Great Depression.* Children's Press, 2007.

Maybury, Rick. *Whatever Happened to Penny Candy?: A Fast, Clear, and Fun Explanation of the Economics You Need for Success in Your Career, Business, and Investments.* Bluestocking Press, 2004.

Reiman, Richard A. *The New Deal and American Youth: Ideas and Ideals in a Depression Decade.* University of Georgia Press, 1992.

Ruth, Amy. *Growing Up in the Great Depression, 1929 to 1941.* Lerner Publications, 2003.

Woolf, Alex. *The Wall Street Crash, October 29, 1929.* Raintree Steck-Vaughn, 2003.

Online Resources:
<http://www.fdrlibrary.marist.edu/gdphotos.html>
   Photos of the Great Depression and the New Deal. Franklin D. Roosevelt Presidential Library and Museum.

<http://memory.loc.gov/ammem/coolhtml/ccpres01.html>
   "The Prosperity of the Coolidge Era." *Prosperity and Thrift: The Coolidge Era and the Consumer Economy, 1921-1929.* The Library of Congress.

<http://memory.loc.gov/learn/lessons/99/edison/gallery.html>
   "Thank You, Mr. Edison: Lesson Three: Merchandising and Advertising: Advertisement Gallery." *The Learning Page.* The Library of Congress.

<http://www.pbs.org/wgbh/amex/rails/timeline/>
   "Timeline of the Great Depression." *Riding the Rails.* Public Broadcasting Service.

<http://kclibrary.nhmccd.edu/decade20.html>
   Whitley, Peggy. *American Cultural History: 1920-1929.* 2006. Kingwood College Library.

Gross Domestic Product

Public vs. Private Goods and Services

Goods and services can be categorized as private or public. **Private goods and services** are provided by businesses and are sold to consumers. Some private goods include books, cars, clothes, computers, and games. A few businesses that provide services include hair salons, theaters, hospitals, and construction companies. The government provides **public goods and services**. Some public goods and services include police protection, national defense, education, and construction and repair of bridges and highways.

GNP vs. GDP

Each year, the nation gets an economic report card. The government calculates the growth of the economy and compares it to the economic growth of past years. The government uses the information to keep the economy healthy and growing.

Before World War I, the United States did not have a set system for computing the economic performance of the nation. No government or private agency was responsible for collecting the data needed to calculate the value of all private and public goods and services produced in a year, or the **gross national product** (**GNP**). In the 1930s, Simon Kuznets, an American economist, developed a method for measuring the yearly economic growth of a nation. In 1971, Kuznets was awarded the Nobel Prize in Economics.

Today, many economists believe using the **gross domestic product** (**GDP**) is a better measure of economic performance than the GNP. The GDP measures the total amount of money spent on private and public goods and services within the United States.

Using GDP Figures

The **Bureau of Economic Analysis** is the agency in the United States Department of Commerce that is responsible for collecting the data used to figure the GDP. The government uses the information to determine which phase of the business cycle the economy is in: expansion, recession, or depression. Economists also use the GDP figures to compare the economic performance of the United States with the economic performance of other countries.

Three major components used in calculating the GDP are household purchases of consumer goods and services, government purchases of goods and services, and purchases of capital goods by businesses: buildings, machinery, and equipment.

Name: _____ Date: _____

Assessment

Matching

_____ 1. public goods and services   a. goods and services provided by the government

_____ 2. private goods and services   b. abbreviation for gross national product

_____ 3. gross domestic product   c. goods and services provided by businesses and sold to consumers

_____ 4. GNP   d. measures the total amount of money spent on private and public goods and services within the United States

Fill in the Blank

1. Goods and services can be categorized as _____ or _____.

2. Some private goods include _____, cars, clothes, _____, and games.

3. The government _____ the growth of the economy and compares it to the economic growth of past years.

4. _____ _____, an American economist, developed a method for measuring the yearly economic growth of a nation.

5. The _____ of _____ Analysis is the agency in the United States Department of Commerce responsible for collecting data to figure the GDP.

6. The government uses the GDP to determine which phase of the business cycle the economy is in: _____, _____, or _____.

Constructed Response

Explain why a society needs both public and private goods and services. Use specific examples and details to support your answer.

_____

_____

_____

_____

Historical Connection

Primary Source:
<http://nobelprize.org/nobel_prizes/economics/laureates/1971/kuznets-autobio.html>
  "Simon Kuznets." *Prize in Economics.* 2008. The Nobel Foundation.

Directions: Simon Kuznets was responsible for developing methods by which nations could measure their gross national products. In 1971, Kuznets was awarded the Nobel Prize in Economics. Using information from the primary source and other sources, students create a time line identifying ten of Kuznets' lifetime achievements.

Knowledge Builder

GDP Comparison of Top Ten Countries

Economists use the Gross Domestic Product (GDP) figure to compare the economic performance of the United States with that of other countries. Students research the following countries to find their GDP: United States, Brazil, Germany, Italy, United Kingdom, Russia, China, Japan, France, and India. They display the information on a world map. Students use the map to draw conclusions about the ten countries with the highest GDPs.

Community Businesses

One indicator of an economically healthy community is the number of businesses located in the area. Students contact their local Chamber of Commerce to find out about business activity over the past decade. Some questions to ask include:

- What is the average number of new businesses started each year?
- What is the average number of businesses that close each year?
- How does the number of businesses ten years ago compare to the number of businesses today?

Students analyze the information to determine business trends in their community.

Public vs. Private

Goods and services can be categorized as private or public. The government provides public goods and services for everyone. Private goods and services are provided by businesses and are sold to consumers. Students identify private and public goods and services available in their community. They select a business or government agency and write a letter requesting an informational brochure. With the information they receive, students create a classroom resource file.

Teacher Resource Bank

National Standards Correlation:

NCEE Standard 18 (Macroecomony-Income/Employment, Prices): A nation's overall levels of income, employment, and prices are determined by the interaction of spending and production decisions made by all households, firms, government agencies, and others in the economy.

NET Standard 5 (Technology Research Tools): Students use technology to locate, evaluate, and collect information from a variety of sources.

Bookshelf Resources:

Gilman, Laura Anne. *Economics.* Lerner Publications, 2006.

Heilbroner, Robert L. and Lester C. Thurow. *Economics Explained: Everything You Need to Know About How the Economy Works and Where It's Going.* 4th ed. Simon & Schuster, 1998.

Kroon, George E. *Macro-economics the Easy Way.* Barron's Educational Series, 2007.

Mayr, Diane. *The Everything Kids' Money Book: From Saving to Spending to Investing—Learn All About Money!* Adams Media, 2000.

Rau, Dana Meachen. *Spending Money.* Weekly Reader Early Learning Library, 2006.

Tillema, Juliana O. *The Young Zillionaire's Guide to Producing Goods and Services.* Rosen Publishing Group, 2000.

Online Resources:

<http://www.econlib.org/LIBRARY/Enc/GrossDomesticProduct.html>
    Anderson, Lincoln. "Gross Domestic Product." *The Library of Economics and Liberty.*

<http://www.quia.com/rd/7615.html>
    Bowermann, Brad. *Top 10 Countries–Gross Domestic Product.* QUIA.

<http://www.investorwords.com/2240/Gross_Domestic_Product.html>
    "Gross Domestic Product." *Business Directory.* 2008. InvestorWords.com.

<http://www.csgnetwork.com/gdpcalc.html>
    "Gross Domestic Product (GDP) Calculator." *Computer Support Group.* 2008. CSGNetwork.Com.

<http://www.bea.gov/national/index.htm#gdp>
    "Gross Domestic Product (GDP)." *National Economic Accounts.* 2007. Bureau of Economic Analysis.

Financing the Government

Revenue

The United States government needs a source of **revenue** or income to pay expenses. Examples of expenses are salaries of elected officials, such as the president and members of Congress. Also, the government pays the salaries of public employees such as soldiers. The government must pay for public goods and services it provides to citizens. **Public goods and services** include national defense, public health services, and education. The revenue comes from a variety of sources, but taxes provide most of the money the government spends. **Taxes** are charges collected from individuals and businesses. State and local governments also collect taxes to pay expenses.

The Power to Levy Taxes

Taxes have been a part of United States history since colonial days. Over-taxation was a major reason the colonists fought for independence from Great Britain. When the United States Constitution was written, the founding fathers realized the new nation needed a way to raise money to finance such items as roads and defense. The writers of the Constitution decided to give Congress the power to levy and to collect taxes.

Types of Taxes

Income Tax
- collected by a city, a state, and/or the federal government
- based on the yearly earnings of individuals or businesses

Property Tax
- collected by a school district, local government, and/or state government
- based on the value of the residential and/or personal property

Sales Tax
- collected by a local and/or state government
- based on the purchase price individuals pay for goods and services

Social Security Tax and Medicare Tax
- collected by the federal government
- paid by workers and employers on wages earned

Progressive vs. Regressive Tax

There are two major classifications of taxes: **progressive** and **regressive**. In a progressive tax, the more individuals earn, the more taxes they pay. An example of a progressive tax is the personal income tax. In a regressive tax, people pay the same amount of tax. An example of a regressive tax is a sales tax. This type of tax affects poor people the most.

Name: _____ Date: _____

Assessment

Matching

_____ 1. revenue

_____ 2. taxes

_____ 3. public goods and services

_____ 4. regressive

_____ 5. progressive

a. provides most of the money government spends

b. the more individuals earn, the more taxes they pay

c. goods and services provided by the government

d. all people pay the same amount of taxes

e. source of income

Fill in the Blank

1. To pay for these expenses, the government needs a source of _____ or revenue.

2. Taxes have been a part of American history since _____ _____.

3. The writers of the Constitution decided to give _____ the power to _____ and to _____ taxes.

4. There are two major classifications of taxes: _____ and _____.

5. An example of a regressive tax is the _____ tax.

Constructed Response

Explain the difference between a progressive and a regressive tax. Use specific examples and details to support your answer.

_____

_____

_____

_____

_____

Historical Connection

Primary Source:
<http://www.tax.org/Museum/images/whiskeytax(small).jpg>
"A Receipt for the Whiskey Tax." *1777-1815: The Revolutionary War to the War of 1812.* Tax History Museum.

Directions: The Constitution gave Congress the power to impose tariffs and coin money. The Whiskey Rebellion of 1794 was the first test of this federal power. In 1791, Congress approved a whiskey excise tax. Unlike the tariff, a tax on imports, the excise tax was a direct tax on American farmers and whiskey producers. Many Americans supported the tax, believing it would cause a reduction in the sales and consumption of alcohol. Others argued it would cause farmers economic hardship and it would hurt trading on the frontier, where whiskey was used as a medium of exchange. Students examine the primary source, a 1798 whiskey tax receipt. Divide the class into two teams: one team for the whiskey tax and one team against the tax. Students research the Whiskey Rebellion and present arguments for their side in the form of a classroom debate.

Knowledge Builder

Social Security History

During the Great Depression, President Franklin D. Roosevelt's New Deal programs created jobs that put people back to work. At first, programs did little to help the elderly. The president appointed Frances Perkins to develop an "old-age" insurance program to assist the elderly. The Social Security Act of 1935 was designed to provide elderly retired workers with an income. Students create a multimedia presentation about the historical background and development of the Social Security System. The Social Security Administration web site (see *Online Resources*) provides a collection of historical related materials, such as the original design of the first Social Security card, pamphlets and posters promoting the program, and a photo gallery of important events and people that will assist students with the project.

Tax Evasion

The deadline for paying personal income tax is April 15th of each year. Taxpayers are legally responsible for preparing and submitting an accurate form called a tax return to the Internal Revenue Service (IRS). Tax evasion, trying to avoid paying taxes, is illegal. Students research the Internal Revenue Service and the legal responsibilities of taxpayers. Using the information, they compose a one- to two-minute public service announcement for the IRS outlining the role of a taxpayer.

Teacher Resource Bank

National Standards Correlation:

<u>NCEE Standard 16 (Role of the Government)</u>: There is an economic role for government in a market economy whenever the benefits of a government policy outweigh its costs. Governments often provide for national defense, address environmental concerns, define and protect property rights, and attempt to make markets more competitive. Most government policies also redistribute income.

<u>NET Standard 5 (Technology Research Tools)</u>: Students use technology to locate, evaluate, and collect information from a variety of sources.

Bookshelf Resources:

Bochner, Arthur and Rose Bochner. *The New Totally Awesome Money Book for Kids! Revised and Updated Edition.* Newmarket Press, 2007.

Giesecke, Ernestine. *Your Money at Work: Taxes.* Heinemann Library, 2003.

Grote, JoAnn A. *The Internal Revenue Service.* Chelsea House Publishing, 2001.

Hamilton, John. *Funding the Nation.* ABDO, 2005.

Macht, Norman L. *Taxes.* Chelsea House Publishing, 2001.

Online Resources:

<http://www.treas.gov/education/fact-sheets/taxes/economics.html>
   "Economics of Taxation." *Fact Sheets: Taxes.* The United States Department of the Treasury.

<http://www.ttb.gov/public_info/whisky_rebellion.shtml>
   Hoover, Michael. *The Whiskey Rebellion.* Alcohol and Tobacco Tax and Trade Bureau.

<http://www.ssa.gov/history/history.html>
   Social Security History. 2008. The Social Security Administration.

<http://www.irs.gov/app/understandingTaxes/jsp/s_student_activities2.jsp>
   "Student Home." *Understanding Taxes.* Internal Revenue Services.

<http://www.taxfoundation.org/taxdata/>
   Tax Data from the Tax Foundation. 2008. Tax Foundation.

<http://www.tax.org/Museum/default.htm>
   Tax History Museum. 2006. Tax History Project.

Income Taxes

The Invention of Income Tax

The first federal income tax was collected in 1862 to help pay the cost of the United States Civil War. Prior to the Civil War, the U.S. government did not tax income; instead, it relied on revenues from **tariffs**, or taxes on imported goods. When the war came to an end, the tax was repealed. The government returned to using tariffs and taxing items such as beer, tobacco, and even chewing gum to raise revenue. Congress realized these types of taxes were not reliable sources of revenue. The Sixteenth Amendment, passed in 1913, gave the government the power to **levy**, or impose and collect, income tax.

Withholding Tax

An **income tax** is a tax on the money an individual or business earns each year. Cities, states, and/or the federal government collect the tax. The government has set up a system of tax withholding to make the payment and collection of personal income taxes more convenient for taxpayers. The employers are responsible for subtracting a certain amount of money from each employee's paycheck and sending it to the appropriate governments.

Pay Day

People are given a pay stub each time they are paid. The pay stub shows details such as how much money has been earned and how much tax has been deducted from the paycheck. The pay stub is a way for the employee to have a record of earnings and deductions.

Filing Tax Returns

The deadline for paying personal income tax is April 15th of each year. Taxpayers are legally responsible for preparing and submitting a tax return to the **Internal Revenue Service** (**IRS**). Many people send their tax returns through the post office. An increasing number of taxpayers use electronic filing because it is faster and more convenient. When the IRS receives the tax return, it is checked for accuracy. **Tax evasion**, trying to avoid paying taxes, is illegal.

As a result of the withholding of taxes, some taxpayers may still owe income tax at the end of the year, while other taxpayers may be entitled to a tax refund. This depends on whether the employer has withheld too little or too much money from an employee's paycheck.

Name: _____ Date: _____

Assessment

Matching

_____ 1. tax evasion

_____ 2. levy

_____ 3. tariff

_____ 4. income tax

_____ 5. IRS

a. Internal Revenue Service

b. trying to avoid paying taxes

c. impose and collect

d. tax on the money an individual or business earns each year

e. tax on imported goods

Fill in the Blank

1. The first federal income tax was collected in _____.

2. The _____ Amendment, passed in 1913, gave the government the power to levy or impose and collect income tax.

3. The _____ _____ shows details such as how much money has been earned and how much tax has been deducted from the paycheck.

4. The deadline for paying personal income tax is _____ _____ each year.

5. Taxpayers are legally responsible for preparing and submitting a tax return to the _____ _____ Service (IRS).

Constructed Response

Explain why some taxpayers owe the government money each year while some taxpayers receive refunds. Use specific examples and details to support your answer.

_____

_____

_____

_____

Historical Connection

Primary Source:
<http://digital.library.unt.edu/permalink/meta-dc-324:1>
"You are one of 50,000,000 Americans who must fill out income tax return by Mar. 15th, file yours early." *Digital Collections.* University of North Texas Libraries.

Directions: The Sixteenth Amendment, passed in 1913, gave the government the power to levy, or impose and collect, income tax. Students examine the primary source, a poster printed in 1944, reminding people to file an income tax return. Students research the reason the deadline for filing income tax returns was changed from March 15th to April 15th. They create a new poster for the IRS reminding people to file their income tax returns by April 15th.

"Article XVI. The Congress shall have power to lay and collect taxes on incomes, from whatever source derived, without apportionment among the several States, and without regard to any census or enumeration."

Knowledge Builder

Exploring Careers

Students research a career they are interested in using the *Occupational Outlook Handbook* web site (see *Online Resources*). The publication provides information such as training, education, earnings, and job responsibilities. To explore occupations, students browse through the handbook's A-Z Index. Using their research, they create a career day presentation.

Pay Day Simulation

Step 1: Students read and discuss the Pay Day page. This page explains the information and vocabulary located on a pay stub.

Step 2: Duplicate the Career Cards page. Cut apart the career cards and have each student randomly draw a card.

Step 3: Using the salary information found on the Career Card and Pay Stub Withholding Table, students construct a bar graph. The graph should show monthly gross salary, net pay, and all tax amounts withheld. Graphs are collected and displayed for students to analyze.

Step 4: Students compare information and draw conclusions about the amount earned and taxes paid.

Step 5: Review with students the definitions for regressive and progressive taxes. Students explain why the income tax is considered a progressive tax.

Pay Day

Employees are given a pay stub each time they are paid. A pay stub shows a person's earnings, the taxes withheld, and other deductions for a specific period of time. The employer is responsible for deducting or subtracting the taxes from an employee's earnings and sending it to the city, state, and/or federal governments. The employee receives a paycheck for the remaining amount of money. The following information appears on most pay stubs.

Gross Salary: the money earned by the employee before taxes and deductions
Federal Income Tax: the money deducted from the gross salary and sent to the federal government
State Income Tax: the money deducted from the gross salary and sent to the state government
OASDI (Old Age, Survivors, and Disability Insurance) or Social Security Tax: the money deducted from the gross salary and sent to the federal government to provide an income for the elderly and retired, families and survivors of the retired, and the disabled
Medicare Tax: the money deducted from the gross salary and sent to the federal government to provide health care for senior citizens over age 65 and the disabled
Net (Take Home) Pay: the employee's pay after all taxes and other deductions have been subtracted from the gross salary

Pay Stub Withholding Table

Yearly Gross Salary	Monthly Gross Salary	Federal Income Tax Withheld Monthly	State Income Tax Withheld Monthly	OASDI (Social Security) Tax Withheld Monthly	Medicare Tax Withheld Monthly	Monthly Net (Take Home) Pay
$10,000	$833.33	$61.25	$7.00	$51.67	$12.08	$701.33
$20,000	$1,666.67	$185.75	$43.00	$103.33	$24.17	$1,310.42
$30,000	$2,500.00	$310.75	$86.00	$155.00	$36.25	$1,912.00
$40,000	$3,333.33	$489.75	$129.00	$206.67	$48.33	$2,459.58
$50,000	$4,166.67	$698.08	$180.00	$258.33	$60.42	$2,969.84
$60,000	$5,000.00	$906.42	$230.00	$310.00	$72.50	$3,481.08
$70,000	$5,833.33	$1,114.75	$279.00	$361.67	$84.58	$3,993.33
$80,000	$6,666.67	$1,330.40	$330.00	$413.33	$96.67	$4,496.27
$90,000	$7,500.00	$1,563.73	$380.00	$465.00	$108.75	$4,982.52
$100,000	$8,333.33	$1,797.06	$429.00	$516.67	$120.83	$5,469.77
$110,000	$9,166.67	$2,030.40	$480.00	$568.33	$132.92	$5,955.02
$120,000	$10,000.00	$2,263.73	$530.00	$620.00	$145.00	$6,441.27
$130,000	$10,833.33	$2,497.06	$579.00	$671.67	$157.08	$6,928.52
$140,000	$11,666.67	$2,730.40	$630.00	$723.33	$169.17	$7,413.77
$150,000	$12,500.00	$2,963.73	$680.00	$755.00	$181.25	$7,900.02

Pay Day Simulation (Continued)

Career Cards

Directions: Duplicate this page. Cut apart and have students randomly draw a Career Card. The dollar amount shown is the yearly gross salary for the occupation.

Accountant $40,000	Biologist $70,000	Restaurant Manager $30,000	Astronomer $90,000
Meteorologist $40,000	Lawyer $90,000	College Professor $70,000	Teacher $40,000
Registered Nurse $50,000	Airline Pilot $140,000	Computer Programmer $50,000	Bank Teller $20,000
Policeman $50,000	Flight Attendant $40,000	Waiter/ Waitress $10,000	Pharmacist $80,000
Pediatrician $130,000	Truck Driver $30,000	Farm Worker $10,000	Dental Assistant $20,000
Architect $60,000	Veterinarian $70,000	Mail Carrier $40,000	Cashier $20,000
Barber/ Cosmetologist $20,000	Physical Therapist $60,000	Secretary $30,000	Automotive Mechanic $30,000

Teacher Resource Bank

National Standards Correlation:

<u>NCEE Standard 16 (Role of the Government)</u>: There is an economic role for government in a market economy whenever the benefits of a government policy outweigh its costs. Governments often provide for national defense, address environmental concerns, define and protect property rights, and attempt to make markets more competitive. Most government policies also redistribute income.

<u>NET Standard 5 (Technology Research Tools)</u>: Students use technology to locate, evaluate, and collect information from a variety of sources.

Bookshelf Resources:

Career Discovery Encyclopedia. Ferguson Publishing Company, 2007.

Giesecke, Ernestine. *Your Money at Work: Taxes.* Heinemann Library, 2003.

Grote, JoAnn A. *The Internal Revenue Service.* Chelsea House Publishing, 2001.

Hamilton, John. *Funding the Nation.* ABDO, 2005.

Macht, Norman L. *Taxes.* Chelsea House Publishing, 2001.

Online Resources:

<http://www.tax.org/Museum/1861-1865.htm>
   "1861-1865: The Civil War." *Tax History Museum.* Tax History Project.

<http://www.treas.gov/education/fact-sheets/taxes/ustax.shtml>
   Fact Sheets: Taxes. U.S. Department of the Treasury.

<http://www.archives.gov/publications/prologue/1986/winter/civil-war-tax-records.html>
   Fox, Cynthia G. "Income Tax Records of the Civil War Years." *Prologue Magazine.* The National Archives.

<http://www.digitalhistory.uh.edu/database/article_display.cfm?HHID=175>
   "Income Tax." *The Progressive Era.* Digital History.

<http://www.irs.gov/>
   Internal Revenue Service. U.S. Department of the Treasury.

<http://www.bls.gov/oco/home.htm>
   Occupational Outlook Handbook. U.S. Department of Labor.

Banking

Early Banking

Banks provide people with a safe place to store their money. In earlier times, people left their coins with money-exchangers and moneylenders who stored the coins in their strongboxes. Later, the idea of banks spread from Italy, where banking was conducted on city street benches, to other European countries. In the 1600s, English goldsmiths acted as bankers. They stored coins for people in their vaults. The goldsmiths issued receipts for the deposits. The receipts or notes were more convenient than coins to carry, so people began using them as money.

United States Banking System

In 1791, the United States Congress established the First Bank of the United States. Many states and individuals also owned and operated banks. During this "Free Banking Era" each bank issued its own bank notes or paper money. Many of the banks printed too much paper money, which led to several financial panics and distrust in the banking system. In 1913, Congress established the Federal Reserve note as the only legal U.S. currency. During the Great Depression of the 1930s, many banks failed. In March of 1933, President Franklin D. Roosevelt ordered a nation-wide bank holiday, the closing of all banks. This stopped people from trying to convert their bank deposits into gold or currency. Roosevelt believed that it would provide time for the "rehabilitation of our banking facilities." Banks that were financially sound were allowed to reopen. **The Federal Deposit Insurance Corporation** (**FDIC**) was created by the United States Congress to help restore faith in the banking industry by protecting a depositor's money.

Banking Today

Today, banks offer a wide variety of services for customers. Money can be **deposited,** or stored, at banks in a variety of accounts. **Checking accounts** allow depositors to withdraw their money through ATMs, debit cards, automatic payment withdrawals, and/or writing checks. Depositors must have enough money in their accounts to cover the money withdrawn. If not, the depositor is penalized with an **overdraft fee**, or charge. **Savings accounts** allow depositors to store their money at the bank. In return, the bank will pay the depositor **interest**, or a fee, for the use of their money. The bank uses the deposited money to make loans to customers. The customers will pay the bank interest on the loan. Also, a bank makes money by charging fees for checking accounts, ATM withdrawals, and overdrafts.

Name: _____   Date: _____

Assessment

Matching

_____ 1. banks   a.   a fee
_____ 2. savings accounts   b.   Federal Deposit Insurance Corporation
_____ 3. deposit   c.   a safe place to store money
_____ 4. interest   d.   allow depositors to store money while earning
                                          interest
_____ 5. FDIC   e.   to store money

Fill in the Blank

1. The idea of banks spread from _____, where banking was conducted
    on city street benches, to other European countries.

2. In 1913, Congress established the _____ _____
    note as the only U.S. currency.

3. In March of 1933, President Franklin D. Roosevelt ordered a nation-wide
    _____ _____, the closing of all banks.

4. _____ _____ allow depositors to withdraw their
    money through ATMs, debit cards, automatic payment withdrawals, and/or writing
    checks.

5. A bank makes money by charging _____ for checking accounts, ATM
    withdrawals, and overdrafts.

Constructed Response

Explain why using an FDIC-insured bank is important to depositors. Give specific examples
and details to support your answer.

_____

_____

_____

_____

Historical Connection

Primary Sources:

<http://www.americanrhetoric.com/speeches/fdrfirstfiresidechat.html>   [Audio Version]
   Roosevelt, Franklin Delano. "The Banking Crisis." *First Fireside Chat.* AmericanRhetoric.
   com.

<http://www.fdrlibrary.marist.edu/031233.html>   [Text Version]
   Roosevelt, Franklin Delano. "On the Bank Crisis." Franklin D. Roosevelt Presidential
   Library and Museum.

Directions: President Franklin Delano Roosevelt (FDR) took office on March 4, 1933. Eight days later, he delivered the first of his radio speeches to U.S. citizens. These radio addresses would become known as "fireside chats." The first chat was on the banking crisis. In the speech, Roosevelt stated, "I want to tell you what has been done in the last few days, and why it was done, and what the next steps are going to be." Students listen to the audio recording of the March 12, 1933, radio address. To facilitate understanding, students follow along with the text version. After listening to the speech, students identify and discuss the steps Roosevelt took to rehabilitate banking facilities.

Knowledge Builder

Banking Services

   Banks offer a wide variety of services for customers. Using a newspaper, students locate advertisements for financial institutions. Then they review several advertisements and create a list of services provided by each bank.

Checking Account Activity

   To be a responsible checking account holder, a depositor must be able to accurately write checks and track all transactions.

Step 1:   Students read and discuss the Checking Account page. The diagrams on that page explain the parts of a check and check register.

Step 2:   Students complete the Check Writing page independently. This page allows students to practice writing a check and recording the information in a check register.

Checking Account

Depositors can withdraw money from their checking account by writing a check. Depositors must keep enough money in their account to cover the checks they write. To make sure that the information on a check cannot be changed or altered, always use a pen, not a pencil.

Parts of a Check

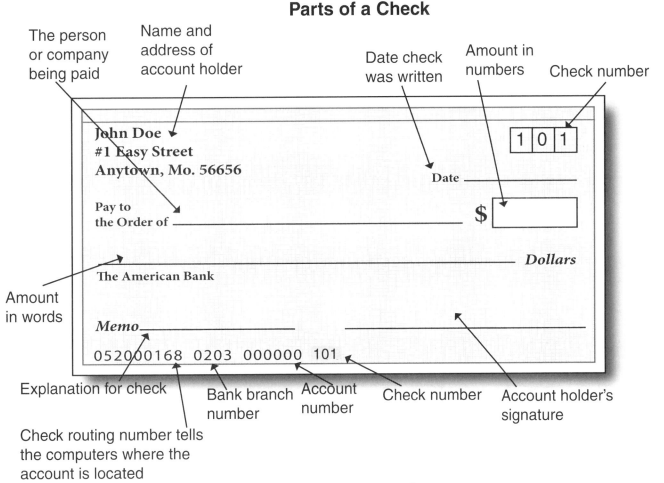

Checkbook Register

A checkbook register is a record of all deposits and withdrawals from a checking account. Deposits are added to the account, and withdrawals are subtracted.

Check Number	Date	Description of Transaction	Payment	Deposit	Balance
					$450.00
101	11/9	Quick Shop	$10.00		10.00
					440.00
	11/30	Deposit		$429.00	429.00
					869.00

Name: _____ Date: _____

Check Writing

Directions: Today, you purchased a pizza from Pizza Palace. The cost of the pizza was $24.95. Using this information, write a check. Fill in your name and address in the box provided.

```
┌─────────────────────────────────────────────────────────────────────┐
│  ┌──────────────────────────┐                          ┌─┬─┬─┐        │
│  │                          │                          │1│0│2│        │
│  │                          │                          └─┴─┴─┘        │
│  │                          │                Date _____       │
│  │                          │                                         │
│  └──────────────────────────┘                           ┌──────────┐  │
│  Pay to                                              $  │          │  │
│  the Order of _____      └──────────┘  │
│                                                                       │
│  _____ Dollars      │
│  The American Bank                                                    │
│                                                                       │
│  Memo_____        _____        │
│  052000168  0203  000000  102                                         │
└─────────────────────────────────────────────────────────────────────┘
```

Check Register

Directions: It is important to keep an accurate record of all deposits to and withdrawals from a checking account. It is illegal to write a check with insufficient funds in the account. Record the following deposit and withdrawal to the register.

1. Record the check to Pizza Palace in the check register and balance the account.
2. Record a deposit of $200.00 and balance the account.

Check Number	Date	Description of Transaction	Payment	Deposit	Balance
					$450.00
101	11/9	Quick Shop	$10.00		10.00
					440.00
	11/30	Deposit		$429.00	429.00
					869.00

Teacher Resource Bank

National Standards Correlation:

NCEE Standard 10: (Role of Economic Institutions): Institutions evolve in market economies to help individuals and groups accomplish their goals. Banks, labor unions, corporations, legal systems, and not-for-profit organizations are examples of important institutions. A different kind of institution, clearly defined and enforced property rights, is essential to a market economy.

NET Standard 5 (Technology Research Tools): Students use technology to locate, evaluate, and collect information from a variety of sources.

Bookshelf Resources:

Allman, Barbara. *Banking.* Lerner Publications, 2006.

Bochner, Arthur and Rose Bochner. *The New Totally Awesome Money Book for Kids! Revised and Updated Edition.* Newmarket Press, 2007.

Giesecke, Ernestine. *Everyday Banking: Consumer Banking.* Heinemann, 2002.

Harman, Hollis Page. *Money Sense for Kids!* Barron's Educational Series, 2004.

Otfinoski, Steve. *The Kid's Guide to Money: Earning It, Saving It, Spending It, Growing It, Sharing It.* Scholastic, 1996.

Online Resources:

<http://www.countrybankforkids.com/kids.htm>
   Country Banks for Kids! Country Bank for Saving.

<http://www.banksite.com/kidscorner/>
   Dollars and Sense for Kids. 2002. BankSITE.

<http://life.familyeducation.com/money-and-kids/personal-finance/34481.html>
   Kids and Money. Family Education.

<http://www.kidsbank.com/index_2.asp>
   KidsBank.com. 2008. Sovereign Bank.

<http://www.moneyopolis.org/new/home.asp>
   Moneyopolis: Where Money Sense Rules! 2003. Ernst & Young LLP.

<http://www.moneyinstructor.com/checks.asp>
   Writing Checks - Checking Account - Checkbook Lessons. MoneyInstructor.com.

Credit Cards

Buying on Credit

Consumers can purchase goods and services without using currency. This is called **buying on credit**. Buying on credit is not a new idea. It dates back to ancient civilizations. Merchants, using a variety of methods, kept records of **debts**, or money owed to them, by customers. One method of early record keeping was tallying using wooden sticks. Tallymen would notch one side of a stick to record the debt and the other side to record payment.

Installment Buying

Credit and debt played a major role in the development of the United States. The invention of the automobile transformed American buying habits. In the early 1900s, Henry Ford produced a low-priced car that people could afford to buy using an installment plan. The **installment plan**, a method of buying on credit with payments over an extended period of time, became a way of life for many people. Later, individual businesses, such as oil companies and hotel chains, would issue credit cards to encourage consumers to shop at their businesses.

Credit Cards

The credit card does not function as money because it cannot act as a unit of accounting and it does not have a store of value. The use of a credit card is a loan from the issuer of the

card. A customer uses a credit card, and the issuer temporarily pays for the customer's purchases. It then sends the customer a statement for all of the charges placed on the credit card that month. The customer can either pay back the card issuer in full or pay only a portion back and be charged interest on the remaining balance. Businesses like to issue credit cards since many consumers do not pay their bills in full every month and end up paying high amounts of interest. An interest rate can vary based on a customer's credit and payment history. Businesses reserve the right to deny credit to any customer that they feel is a bad risk or might not be able to repay the debt.

Problems With Buying on Credit

Buying on credit can be a convenient way to shop for consumers. Unfortunately, credit cards are not free money. They are high-interest loans. The availability of easy credit encourages people to spend more money than they can afford. High interest rates on credit card balances can cause people's debts to accumulate rapidly. Late or missed payments on a credit card are reported to credit bureaus. This will lower an individual's **credit rating**, which is used to determine whether or not a person is a good credit risk.

Name: _____ Date: _____

Assessment

Matching

_____ 1. credit
_____ 2. debts
_____ 3. installment plan
_____ 4. credit rating

a. purchase goods and services without using currency
b. used to determine whether or not a person is a good credit risk
c. money owed
d. method of buying on credit with payments over an extended period of time

Fill in the Blank

1. _____ would notch one side of a stick to record the debt and the other side to record payment.

2. _____ _____ produced a low-priced car that people could afford to buy on credit using an installment plan.

3. The credit card does not function as _____ because it cannot act as a unit of accounting and does not have a store of value.

4. The use of a credit card is a _____ from the issuer of the card.

5. High _____ _____ on credit card balances can cause people's debts to accumulate rapidly.

6. Late or missed payments on a credit card are reported to _____ _____.

Constructed Response

Explain how late or missed credit card payments can damage your credit rating. Give specific examples and details to support your answer.

_____
_____
_____
_____
_____

Historical Connection

Primary Source:
<http://hdl.loc.gov/loc.mss/amrlm.mc09>
"Credit—Installment Plan Buying 1926-29." *Calvin Coolidge Papers.* The Library of Congress.

Directions: The 1920s was an era of great prosperity. In January of 1926, newspaper advertisements included a statement made by President Coolidge endorsing installment buying. At this time, many people felt that installment buying destroyed a person's character and could lead to a nation's economic downfall. Following the publication of the advertisements, communications from individuals and businesses flooded the White House. They were either attacking Coolidge's point of view or expressing an interest in his opinion. Students access the primary source web site and select image 2, a letter and newspaper clippings from P. A. Lovewell, the vice-president and editor of the *Merchant Journal*. Then they select images 47 and 48, an advertisement encouraging installment buying. Students examine the primary sources to gain a better understanding of the feelings of people of the 1920s in regard to buying on the installment plan. They write a letter to President Coolidge from the perspective of a person who supports buying on credit.

Knowledge Builder

Chargers Beware

Most of the responsibility of having and using a credit card falls on the credit card holder. There are several "rules" or guidelines for credit card usage that should be followed by every credit card holder. In the 1920s, the Young Men's Christian Association (YMCA) had ten financial commandments as the foundation of its National Thrift Program. To view these ten financial commandments, follow these steps.

Step 1: Access the following web site:
<http://hdl.loc.gov/loc.mss/amrlm.mk03>
Anna Kelton Wiley Papers. Homemaker-Consumer Life in Washington, D.C., 1922-23. The Library of Congress.
Step 2: Click on "View this Item."
Step 3: Scroll down and click on "Page Images."
Step 4: Click on "Next Image" until image 12 is displayed.

Using a similar format to the ten financial commandments, students create an informational brochure listing ten financial rules that encourages the responsible use of credit cards.

Teacher Resource Bank

National Standards Correlation:

NCEE Standard 3 (Allocation of Goods and Services): Different methods can be used to allocate goods and services. People, acting individually or collectively through government, must choose which methods to use to allocate different kinds of goods and services.

NET Standard 5 (Technology Research Tools): Students use technology to locate, evaluate, and collect information from a variety of sources.

Bookshelf Resources:

Basel, Roberta. *Checks, Credit, and Debit Cards.* Capstone Press, Inc., 2006.

Bochner, Arthur and Rose Bochner. *The New Totally Awesome Money Book for Kids! Revised and Updated Edition.* Newmarket Press, 2007.

Cooper, Jason. *Paying Without Money.* Rourke Publishing Group, 2002.

Giesecke, Ernestine. *Dollars and Sense: Managing Your Money.* Heinemann Library, 2003.

Green, Meg. *Everything You Need to Know About Credit Cards and Fiscal Responsibility.* Rosen Publishing Group, 2001.

Hall, Margaret. *Credit Cards and Checks.* Heinemann Library, 2001.

Minden, Cecilia. *Using Credit Wisely.* Cherry Lake Publishing, 2008.

Online Resources:

<http://www.moneyinstructor.com/creditcards.asp>
   Credit Card Lessons. MoneyInstructor.com.

<http://money.howstuffworks.com/credit-card1.htm>
   How Credit Cards Work. 2006. HowStuffWorks.

<http://www.econedlink.org/lessons/index.cfm?lesson=EM346>
   "Q T Pi Fashions – Learning About Credit Card Use." *EconEdlink.* 2007. National Council on Economic Education.

<http://www.pbs.org/wgbh/pages/frontline/shows/credit/>
   "Secret History of the Credit Card." *Frontline.* 2004. Public Broadcasting Service.

Investment

Saving is setting aside income for future use. Some reasons for saving money are for an emergency, a major purchase, education, vacation, and/or retirement. When many people think of saving, they think of putting money in a savings account where it will earn interest. Today, people have many options when investing their money. Before investing, it is important to understand the types of investments and their risk factors.

Types of Investment	Descriptions	Risk Factor (RF)
Savings Account	The investor deposits money in a safe place (bank, credit union, or savings and loan association) while earning interest. **Interest** is a fee paid to the investor so the money can be used to fund loans.	Banks insure deposits through the **Federal Deposit Insurance Corporation** (**FDIC**). This means if an FDIC-insured bank fails, depositors will get up to the first $100,000 of their deposits back. **RF: None**
Certificate of Deposit (CD)	The investor earns a higher rate of interest by depositing money in an account at a bank or credit union. CDs have a **maturity date**, the date when the investor can cash in a CD without a **penalty**, or fee.	The FDIC protects Certificates of Deposits purchased through a bank. **RF: None**
Government Bonds, Corporate Bonds, and Municipal Bonds	The purchaser of a bond is really loaning money to the bond issuer. Upon the bond's maturity, the investor receives a fixed amount of interest along with the initial investment.	The federal government backs government bonds. They pay a fixed amount of interest. **RF: None** Corporate and municipal bonds are a riskier investment because of possible default by the bond issuer and changing interest rates. **RF: Low Risk**
Stocks	The investor buys shares of ownership in a company, anticipating that the stock will increase in value. There is always the risk that the stock will decrease in value. If the stock is sold at a higher value, then the investor has made a capital gain.	If the company is not successful, shares or stocks will be worth less than the original purchase price. Selling them will result in a capital loss instead of a capital gain. **RF: High Risk**
Mutual Funds	The investor becomes a member of a group of investors with a professional fund manager who purchases and sells stocks and bonds on behalf of the group.	Mutual funds are vulnerable to the same risk factors as stocks and bonds. Also, the fund manager may not invest the funds wisely. **RF: High Risk**

Name: _____　Date: _____

Assessment

Matching

_____ 1. saving

_____ 2. maturity date

_____ 3. penalty

_____ 4. interest

_____ 5. FDIC

a. Federal Deposit Insurance Corporation

b. the date when the investor can cash in a CD without a penalty

c. fee paid to the investor so the money can be used to fund loans

d. fee

e. setting aside income for future use

Fill in the Blank

1. The investor earns a higher rate of _____ by depositing money in a certificate of deposit account at a bank or credit union.

2. The purchaser of a bond is really _____ money to the bond issuer.

3. Upon the bond's maturity, the investor receives a _____ amount of interest along with the initial investment.

4. _____ and _____ bonds are a riskier investment because of possible default by the bond issuer and changing interest rates.

5. _____ funds are vulnerable to the same risks as stocks and bonds.

Constructed Response

Explain why investing in stocks is riskier than a savings accounts. Give specific examples and details to support your answer.

_____

_____

_____

_____

_____

Historical Connection

Primary Source:
<http://content.lib.washington.edu/cgi-bin/htmlview.exe?CISOROOT=/loc&CISOPTR=1102>
"Colville student, Willie Warren's original math problem, Fort Spokane, Washington." *Digital Collections.* University of Washington Libraries.

Directions: Students visit the web site and solve the original problem on calculating interest that is found in the primary source. The problem was created by twelve-year-old Willie Warren. After solving the problem, students examine the primary source to compare their answer to Willie Warren's solution.

Knowledge Builder

United States Savings Bonds

Government savings bonds are a risk-free investment. The current bond program was introduced in 1935. One of the purposes of this bond program was to provide an opportunity for investors with limited capital. Students explore the web site below and answer the following questions on their own paper about the United States Savings Bond program.

<http://www.publicdebt.treas.gov/sav/savlearn.htm>
"Learn." 2002. Bureau of the Public Debt.

Questions:
1. What is the definition of a savings bond?
2. What are three reasons people purchase savings bonds?
3. Name two places where savings bonds can be purchased.
4. Where can savings bonds be redeemed?

Piggy Banks

One of the first tools for saving money was a piggy bank. It is commonly believed that the first piggy banks were made from clay called pygg. Students research the history of piggy banks. Each student creates a piggy bank using the directions found on the web site listed below:

<http://www.enchantedlearning.com/crafts/Piggybank.shtml>
"Piggy Bank." 2007. Enchanted Learning.com.

Teacher Resource Bank

National Standards Correlation:

NCEE Standard 12 (Role of Interest Rates): Interest rates, adjusted for inflation, rise and fall
to balance the amount saved with the amount borrowed, which affects the allocation of
scarce resources between present and future uses.

NET Standard 5 (Technology Research Tools): Students use technology to locate, evaluate,
and collect information from a variety of sources.

Bookshelf Resources:

Bailey, Gerry. *Get Rich Quick?: Earning Money.* Compass Point Books, 2006.

Barbash, Fred. *Investing Your Money: Exploring Business and Economics.* Chelsea House
Publications, 2001.

Bateman, Katherine. *The Young Investor: Projects and Activities for Making Your Money Grow.*
Chicago Review Press, 2001.

Gardner, David and Tom Gardner. *The Motley Fool Investment Guide for Teens: Eight Steps to
Having More Money Than Your Parents Ever Dreamed Of.* Simon & Schuster, 2002.

Karlitz, Gail. *Growing Money: A Complete (and Completely Updated!) Investing Guide for Kids.*
Price Stern Sloan, 2001.

Minden, Cecilia. *Investing: Making Your Money Work for You.* Cherry Lake Publishing, 2008.

Online Resources:

<http://www.themint.org/kids/investing.html>
    "Investing." *The Mint: It Makes Perfect Cents.* 2007. Northwestern Mutual.

<http://www.publicdebt.treas.gov/sav/savlearn.htm>
    "Learn." 2002. United States Department of the Treasury/Bureau of the Public Debt.

<http://www.moneyopolis.org/new/home.asp>
    Moneyopolis: Where Money Sense Rules. 2003. Ernst & Young LLP.

<http://pbskids.org/itsmylife/money/managing/index.html>
    "Spending and Saving." *Managing Money.* 2005. PBSKids.

<http://www.younginvestor.com/>
    Younginvestor.com. 2007. Columbia Management.

Stock Market

Stock Market Terminology

The **stock market** is a place where people can buy, sell, or trade **stocks**, or shares of ownership in companies. A company sells shares to raise money for expansion or research for product development. People who buy stocks are investing in the company. They become **stockholders**, or part owners in the company with the hope of making money. If the company grows and makes a profit, the investor can make money. The company may share the profits with the stockholder by paying a **dividend**. The stockholder can also make money or a capital gain by selling the stock when the price per share increases. Stockholders often pay stockbrokers to manage their stock **portfolio**, which are all the stocks an investor owns. Investing in the stock market is risky, and profits are not guaranteed.

History of the U.S. Stock Market

The United States emerged from the American Revolution as a nation heavily in debt. The founding fathers wanted to pay off war debt while becoming an economic world power. Alexander Hamilton, the first U.S. Secretary of the Treasury, came up with the idea of starting a stock exchange modeled after the one in Great Britain. In New York, selling stocks became so successful that the stock market trading moved from a street corner into a building on Wall Street.

The stock market prospered in the United States until the early 1900s. Individuals hoping to become millionaires were borrowing large sums from banks to buy stocks. Investing in stocks made fortunes. By the fall of 1929, heavy speculation, which is buying, selling, and trading of stocks on credit, had driven stock prices to record highs. When stock prices started to fall, it caused a nationwide panic. Investors rushing to sell found no one wanting to buy. In late October, the stock market crashed. The crash was a major cause of the Great Depression. The Securities Act of 1933 established the Securities and Exchange Commission to protect investors and the nation against another stock market crash. Today, the stock market is monitored and regulated at both the state and federal levels.

Tracking Stocks

Stocks are traded on a variety of stock exchanges throughout the world. One of the largest and most familiar exchanges is the New York Stock Exchange (NYSE). One of the most popular ways to keep track of the up and down movement of the entire stock market is to check the Dow Jones  Industrial Average (DOW). Two animals are used to describe  the ups and downs of the stock market. A **bull market** is when stock market prices continue to rise over an extended time period. A **bear market** is the opposite of a bull market.

Name: _____ Date: _____

Assessment

Matching

_____ 1. stock market

_____ 2. stocks

_____ 3. stockholders

_____ 4. portfolio

_____ 5. bull market

a. all of the stocks an investor owns

b. a market where people can buy, sell, or trade stocks

c. shares of ownership in companies

d. part owners in the company

e. when stock market prices rise over an extended time period

Fill in the Blank

1. The company may share the profits with the stockholder by paying a _____.

2. Investing in the stock market is _____, and profits are not guaranteed.

3. _____ _____, the first U.S. Secretary of the Treasury, modeled the stock exchange after the one in Great Britain.

4. The _____ _____ of 1933 established the Securities and Exchange Commission to protect investors and the nation against another stock market crash.

5. One of the largest and most familiar exchanges is the _____ _____ Stock Exchange (NYSE).

Constructed Response

Explain why investing in the stock market can be risky. Give specific examples and details to support your answer.

_____

_____

_____

_____

_____

Historical Connection

Primary Sources:
<http://www.bl.uk/learning/images/front%20page/Wall-Street-lg.jpg>
    "Greatest Crash in Wall Street History." British Library.

<http://www.nytimes.com/learning/general/onthisday/big/1029.html#article>
    "Stocks Collapse in 16,410,030-Share Day, But Rally at Close Cheers Brokers; Bankers Optimistic to Continue Aide." *The New York Times.*

Directions: The dramatic fall of stock prices in 1929, and the financial panic that followed, affected nations around the world. Newspaper headlines captured everyone's attention on the day after the crash. Students read and analyze the primary sources. They compare and contrast the perspectives of the two newspaper articles. Students report their findings to the class using a graphic organizer.

Knowledge Builder

Stock Market Simulation

Step 1: Students read and discuss the *Reading a Stock Table* page. This page provides explanations and vocabulary for interpreting the information found on a stock table. They complete the *Reading a Stock Table Assessment* page to check comprehension.

Step 2: Divide the class into groups of four or five. Each group chooses a team name. Teams brainstorm and compile a list of companies with which they are familiar. The following questions will help students compile their list.
- Which brands of soda do they like?
- Which brands of electronics do they own?
- Which brands of clothing do they wear?
- Which brands of breakfast cereal or snacks do they eat?

Step 3: Teams research companies on their list to find out the company's ticker symbol and key company information. The Internet web site below will help the students with their research. (Hint: Use only the NYSE for this simulation.)

<http://www.nyse.com/about/listed/name.html?ListedComp=All>
    Listed Company Directory. New York Stock Exchange.

Step 4: Each team has an imaginary $10,000 to purchase stocks for the simulation. Using their research, each team selects five companies for their investment portfolio. They purchase $2,000 of stock in each of the five companies. Using the stock table in the financial section of the newspaper or the New York Stock Exchange web site, teams track their stocks. Teams use the Stock Market Game Tracking Record pages to record the movement of their stocks over an eight-week period. At the end of the eight weeks, the team with the most money in their portfolio is the winner.

Reading A Stock Table

An easy way to track stocks is through a newspaper. Stock information is usually found using the stock table located in the financial section of most newspapers. Stocks are traded on a variety of stock exchanges in the United States. A stockholder needs to know under which exchange their stock is listed. The largest and most familiar exchange in the world is the **New York Stock Exchange** (**NYSE**). This exchange lists stocks for large established companies. The **American Stock Exchange** (**AMEX**) lists stocks for smaller or newer companies. The **National Association of Security Dealers Automated Quotations System** (**NASDAQ**) lists stocks for high-technology companies.

One of the popular ways to keep track of the up and down movement of the entire stock market is to check the **Dow Jones Industrial Average** (**DOW**). Below is an example of some of the information found in a stock table.

Column: 1		2	3	4	5	6
52 Week		**Stock, Symbol (SYM), or Name**	**Split (s)**	**Year to Date (YTD)**	**Close or Last**	**Change (Chg)**
High	**Low**					
14.00	4.15	ARZ		−47.70	4.71	+0.20
39.29	8.70	AAL		−61.70	12.49	−0.17
42.88	28.92	Bk Tw		+10.00	13.10	−0.40
53.75	18.50	BBB	s	+12.90	46.64	−0.84
59.99	36.33	KAT		+28.80	19.25	+0.35
7.10	3.25	CTM		+20.10	21.09	−0.34

Column 1: **52 Week High/Low** reports the stock's high and low selling price over the past year.

Column 2: **Stock, Symbol (SYM), or Name** reports the stock's name, abbreviated version of the stock's name, or the ticker symbol used on the exchange.

Column 3: **Split (s)** reports a stock split. The stocks have been divided into a larger number of lower priced shares. Example: If a $10.00 share is split 2 for 1, the stockholder ends up with two shares each worth $5.00.

Column 4: **Year to Date (YTD)** reports % of change in the stock's price either up (+) or down (−) over a year.

Column 5: **Close or Last** reports the price the stock was selling for at the end of that trading day.

Column 6: **Change (Chg)** reports the change in a stock's price either up (+) or down (−) on that particular trading day.

Name: _____ Date: _____

Reading A Stock Table Assessment

Matching

_____ 1. DOW

_____ 2. AMEX

_____ 3. NASDAQ

_____ 4. NYSE

a. exchange that lists stocks for high-technology companies

b. exchange that lists stocks for large, established companies

c. exchange that lists stocks for smaller and newer companies

d. tracks the up and down movement of the entire stock market

Fill in the Blank

Use the stock table on page 83 to answer the questions below.

1. What was the closing price for AAL? _____

2. Which stock had a split? _____

3. Does the change in ARZ stock price indicate a loss (–) or gain (+) in the price of the stock

   for the day? _____

Constructed Response

1. Looking at the last three columns on the stock table, why is KAT a good choice for investment? Explain your answer giving specific details.

   _____

   _____

   _____

   _____

2. Looking at the last three columns on the stock table, why is AAL not a good choice for investment? Explain your answer giving specific details.

   _____

   _____

   _____

   _____

Name: _____ Date: _____

Stock Market Tracking Record

Week One: Building a Stock Portfolio

Directions:

1. Using the *Week One: Tracking Chart*, list the stock symbols for the five stocks your team has selected.

2. Using the financial page of the newspaper, locate each of the stocks in your portfolio. Look at the *Closing or Last* column on the stock table. This column indicates the selling price of each stock. Find each stock's selling price. Record the price under the *Price Per Share* column on the *Week One: Tracking Chart*.

3. Your team is investing $2,000 in each stock. This amount has already been entered under the *Value of Individual Stock Investment* column.

4. Calculate the number of shares your team was able to purchase for each stock using the following formula:

Formula: $\dfrac{\text{Investment Value}}{\text{Price Per Share}} = \text{\# of Shares}$ Example: $\dfrac{\$2000.00}{\$39.98} = 50.02 \text{ shares}$

5. Record the number of shares you were able to purchase in the *Number of Shares* column. (Do not round answers. Drop all numbers beyond the hundredths place.)

6. The *Total Portfolio Value* row indicates the total value of your team's stock portfolio. At the beginning of the simulation, the total value of your team's stock portfolio is $10,000.

Week One: Tracking Chart

Stock	Price Per Share	Number of Shares	Value of Individual Stock Investment
			$2000.00
			$2000.00
			$2000.00
			$2000.00
			$2000.00
Total Portfolio Value			$10,000.00

Name: _____ Date: _____

Stock Market Tracking Record (cont.)

Week Two

Directions:

1. Transfer stock symbols and number of shares from the previous week's tracking chart to the new chart.

2. Using the financial page of the newspaper, locate each of the stocks in your portfolio. Look at the *Closing or Last* column on the stock table. This column indicates the selling price of each stock. Record the price under the *Price Per Share* column on the new tracking chart.

3. Calculate the new investment values for each individual stock. Multiply the stock's price per share and number of shares. Record the answer in the *Value of Individual Stock Investment* column.

4. To find the new value of your team's stock portfolio, add the numbers in the *Value of Individual Stock Investment* column. Record the answer on the *Total Portfolio Value* row.

Week Two: Tracking Chart

Stock	Price Per Share	Number of Shares	Value of Individual Stock Investment
Total Portfolio Value			

Name: _____   Date: _____

Stock Market Tracking Record (cont.)

Tracking Stocks

Directions: Duplicate this page to record stocks for weeks three through eight. Complete the charts using the directions for Week Two.

Week _____: Tracking Chart

Stock	Price Per Share	Number of Shares	Value of Individual Stock Investment
Total Portfolio Value			

Week _____: Tracking Chart

Stock	Price Per Share	Number of Shares	Value of Individual Stock Investment
Total Portfolio Value			

Name: _____ Date: _____

Stock Market Portfolio Assessment

Directions: Answer the following questions about your stock market portfolio.

1. Did your team's stock portfolio make a capital gain or capital loss? Give specific examples and details to support your answer.

   _____

   _____

   _____

   _____

2. List two of the best performing stocks in your portfolio. Explain why they were the best stock choices.

   _____

   _____

   _____

   _____

3. In your opinion, was your team's $10,000 investment a wise economic decision? Explain your answer. Use examples from the tracking charts to support your answer.

   _____

   _____

   _____

   _____

4. You have $5,000 to invest. Based on the experience gained from the Stock Market Simulation, would you deposit the entire amount in your savings account or invest it in the stock market? Give specific examples and details to support your answer.

   _____

   _____

   _____

   _____

Teacher Resource Bank

National Standards Correlation:

NCEE Standard 15 (Growth): Investment in factories, machinery, new technology, and in the health, education, and training of people can raise future standards of living.

NET Standard 5 (Technology Research Tools): Students use technology to locate, evaluate, and collect information from a variety of sources.

Bookshelf Resources:

Davidson, Avelyn. *The Bull and the Bear: How Stock Markets Work.* Children's Press, 2007.

Doak, Robin S. *Black Tuesday: Prelude to the Great Depression.* Compass Point Books, 2007.

Fuller, Donna Jo. *The Stock Market.* Lerner Publications, 2005.

McGowan, Eileen Nixon and Nancy Lagow Dumas. *Stock Market Smart.* Millbrook Press, 2002.

Woolf, Alex. *The Wall Street Crash, October 29, 1929.* Raintree Steck-Vaughn, 2003.

Online Resources:

<http://memory.loc.gov/ammem/today/jul08.html>
    "George Mehales. Spartanburg, South Carolina, R. V. Williams, interviewer, December 1938, American Live Histories: manuscripts from the Federal Writers' project, 1936-1940." *Today in History, July 8.* 2007. The Library of Congress.

<http://www.nyse.com/about/history/1089312755484.html>
    History. NYSE.

<http://www.ohiohistorycentral.org/entry.php?rec=559>
    Stock Market Crash of 1929. 2008. Ohio Historical Society.

<http://library.thinkquest.org/3088/stockmarket/introduction.html>
    The Stock Market. Think Quest.

<http://www.americaslibrary.gov/cgi-bin/page.cgi/jb/wwii/stockmrkt_2>
    "The Stock Market Fell to Its Lowest Point During the Depression July 8, 1932." *America's Story from America's Library.* The Library of Congress.

<http://www.eyewitnesstohistory.com/snpmech5.htm>
    "The Wall Street Crash, 1929." *America in the 20s.* EyeWitness to History.

Answer Keys

Bartering (page 3)
Matching:
1. b   2. c   3. a

Fill in the Blanks:
1. surplus   2. Hudson Bay
3. Continental Army   4. Manhattan
5. Lewis, Clark

Constructed Response:
Bartering is the trading of items people have for items they want. In order to save money, companies and individuals have discovered the convenience of online bartering.

History of Money (page 10)
Matching:
1. c   2. d   3. a   4. b

Fill in the Blanks:
1. bartering   2. commodity   3. Chinese
4. Massachusetts   5. continentals
6. Federal Reserve

Constructed Response:
The United States needs a legal tender that will be accepted in all 50 states. Trade between states would be difficult with 50 different currencies. The danger of states issuing too much money is that the currency would become worthless.

United States Currency (page 14)
Matching:
1. d   2. c   3. b   4. a

Fill in the Blanks:
1. Constitution   2. Alexander Hamilton
3. "P"   4. Federal Reserve
5. 1, 2, 100

Constructed Response:
The United States Mint is the federal agency responsible for the design and production of coins. The Bureau of Engraving and Printing is the federal agency responsible for designing, engraving, and printing Federal Reserve notes.

Features of Money (page 19)
Matching:
1. d   2. e   3. a
4. b   5. c

Fill in the Blanks:
1. security, counterfeiting
2. medium, exchange
3. save
4. color
5. embedded, ultraviolet
6. United States, America

Constructed Response:
People would not accept rocks as a medium of exchange. The value of rocks has not been established. They are not convenient to carry around. They are not scarce. They are not easily divided into equal parts. They are not durable because they are easily chipped.

Economics (page 25)
Matching:
1. d   2. e   3. b
4. c   5. a

Fill in the Blanks:
1. bought, sold   2. products
3. teachers, cooks, lawyers, bankers, comedians, nurses
4. raw   5. money, time

Constructed Response:
Scarcity of resources means individuals, businesses, and nations will never have all the goods and services they want.

Factors of Production (page 29)
Matching:
1. b   2. d   3. e
4. c   5. a

Fill in the Blanks:
1. factors of production   2. rent
3. wages   4. Capitalism   5. profit

Constructed Response:
Answers will vary.

Supply and Demand (page 33)

Matching:
1. b   2. e   3. f
4. a   5. d   6. c

Fill in the Blanks:
1. increase   2. tobacco
3. skyrocketed   4. nonrenewable

Constructed Response:
The price of coats increases in the winter because there is an increase in demand. The price of coats decreases in the summer because there is a decrease in demand.

Opportunity Cost and Trade-offs (page 37)

Fill in the Blanks:
1. trade-offs   2. Trade-offs
3. opportunity cost 4. entrepreneurs
5. advertising, remodeling, wages

Constructed Response:
Answers will vary.

Economic Systems (page 41)

Matching:
1. b   2. a   3. d
4. c   5. e

Fill in the Blanks:
1. United States   2. profits
3. customs   4. quotas

Constructed Response:
Advantages and disadvantages will vary.
Market: free enterprise system where consumers
    and producers make the decisions
    (Example country: United States)
Traditional: economic decisions are based on a
    society's customs, culture, and way of life
    (Example country: Ethiopia)
Command: government makes economic
    decisions and owns most industries
    (Example country: North Korea)

Organization of Business (page 45)

Matching:
1. c   2. a   3. b
4. d   5. e

Fill in the Blanks:
1. size, owners
2. Andrew Carnegie, Sam Walton
3. owner
4. partnership
5. capital

Constructed Response:
The owner makes all the business decisions: what to produce or sell, how much to charge customers, and what hours to work. The owner receives all the profits if the business is successful.

The Business Cycle (page 49)

Matching:
1. e   2. c   3. b
4. a   5. d

Fill in the Blanks:
1. growing, expanding   2. inflation
3. booming   4. stock market
5. monitors, regulates

Constructed Response:
Competition for goods and services causes inflation or prices to increase. People have to spend more for goods and services, so they are able to buy less.

Gross Domestic Product (page 53)

Matching:
1. a   2. c   3. d   4. b

Fill in the Blanks:
1. private, public   2. books, computers
3. calculates   4. Simon Kuznets
5. Bureau, Economic
6. expansion, recession, depression

Constructed Response:
Private goods and services are the everyday things that people need and businesses provide. Prices are influenced by supply and demand. Public goods and services are provided to everyone by the government. They are paid for by taxes. Public goods and services allow citizens to have access to things they need but would not be able to afford as an individual, such as national defense, highways, and police protection.

Financing the Government (page 57)
Matching:
1. e   2. a   3. c
4. d   5. b

Fill in the Blanks:
1. income
2. colonial days
3. Congress, levy, collect
4. progressive, regressive
5. sales

Constructed Response:
In a progressive tax, the more individuals earn, the more taxes they pay. An example of a progressive tax is the personal income tax. In a regressive tax, all people pay the same amount of tax. An example of a regressive tax is a sales tax.

Income Taxes (page 61)
Matching:
1. b   2. c   3. e
4. d   5. a

Fill in the Blanks:
1. 1862   2. Sixteenth
3. pay stub   4. April 15th
5. Internal Revenue

Constructed Response:
Employers are responsible for withholding, or subtracting, a certain amount of money from each employee's paycheck and sending it to the appropriate government. As a result of the withholding of taxes, some taxpayers may still owe income tax at the end of the year, while other taxpayers may be entitled to a tax refund. This depends on whether the employer has withheld too little or too much money from an employee's paycheck.

Banking (page 67)
Matching:
1. c   2. d   3. e
4. a   5. b

Fill in the Blanks:
1. Italy   2. Federal Reserve
3. bank holiday   4. Checking accounts
5. fees

Constructed Response:
If an FDIC-insured bank fails, depositors will get up to the first $100,000 of their deposit back.

Credit Cards (page 73)
Matching:
1. a   2. c   3. d   4. b

Fill in the Blanks:
1. Tallymen   2. Henry Ford
3. money   4. loan
5. interest rates   6. credit bureaus

Constructed Response:
Late or missed credit card payments are reported to credit bureaus. This will lower an individual's credit rating. Credit ratings are used to determine whether or not a person is a good credit risk.

Investment (page 77)
Matching:
1. e   2. b   3. d
4. c   5. a

Fill in the Blanks
1. interest   2. loaning
3. fixed   4. Corporate, municipal
5. Mutual

Constructed Response:
Banks insure deposits through the Federal Deposit Insurance Corporation (FDIC). This means if an FDIC-insured bank fails, depositors will get up to the first $100,000 of their deposits back. When investing in stocks, the investor is buying shares of ownership in a company. If the company is not successful, stocks will be worth less than the original purchase prices. The FDIC does not cover losses in the stock market.

Stock Market (page 81)
Matching:
1. b   2. c   3. d
4. a   5. e

Fill in the Blanks:
1. dividend   2. risky
3. Alexander Hamilton   4. Securities Act
5. New York

Constructed Response:
People who buy stocks are investing in a company. If the company grows and makes a profit, the investor can make money. The company might pay a dividend to the stockholder. Stockholders can sell stock when the price per share increases. If the company is not successful, there is always the risk the stock will decrease in value and the investor will lose money.

Reading a Stock Table (page 84)
Matching:
1. d   2. c   3. a   4. b

Fill in the Blanks:
1. $12.49   2. BBB   3. gain

Constructed Response:
1. The YTD column indicates the stock increased in value 28.80% over the year. The Chg column indicates the stock's price increased $0.35 that trading day.
2. The YTD column indicates the stock decreased in value 61.70% over the year. The Chg column indicates the stock price decreased $0.17 that trading day.

Stock Market Portfolio (page 88)
Answers to the questions will vary depending on the performance of each team's stock portfolio.

Bibliography

Biedenweg, Karl. *Basic Economics.* Quincy, Illinois: Mark Twain Media, Inc. 1999.

Biedenweg, Karl. *Understanding Investment & The Stock Market.* Quincy, Illinois: Mark Twain Media, Inc. 2003.

Burger, James P. *Mountain Men of the West.* New York: PowerKids Press, 2002.

De Rooy, Jacob. *Economic Literacy: What Everyone Needs to Know About Money & Markets.* New York: Three Rivers Publishing, 1996.

Doak, Robin S. *Black Tuesday: Prelude to the Great Depression.* Minneapolis, Minnesota: Compass Point Books, 2007.

Golomb, Kristen Girard. *Economics and You.* Quincy, Illinois: Mark Twain Media, Inc. 1996.

"Know Your Money: History of United States Currency." *United States Secret Service.* 2006. United States Secret Service. 11 Oct. 2007 <http://www.secretservice.gov/money_history.shtml>.

Saffell, David C. *Civics: Responsibilities and Citizenship.* New York: Glencoe/McGraw-Hill, 2002.

"Treasury History Overview." *Office of the Curator.* 12 Mar. 2007. United States Department of the Treasury. 9 Oct. 2007 <http://www.treas.gov/education/history/brochure>.